GEORGE A. ROMERO

ON SCREEN

2020 EDITION

By Chris Wade

GEORGE A. ROMERO ON SCREEN 2020 EDITION

by Chris Wade

Wisdom Twins Books, 2020

wisdomtwinsbooks.weebly.com

This edition released in 2020

Text Copyright of Chris Wade

GEORGE A. ROMERO

ON SCREEN

THEY WON'T STAY DEAD!

An IMAGE TEN Production

NIGHT OF THE LIVING DEAD

They keep coming back in a
bloodthirsty lust for
HUMAN FLESH!...
Pits the dead against the living
in a struggle for survival!

Starring JUDITH O'DEA · DUANE JONES · MARILYN EASTMAN · KARL HARDMAN · JUDITH RIDLEY · KEITH WAYNE

INTRODUCTION

There are a number of striking filmic images which define the horror genre with simplicity and starkness. Think the shower scene in Alfred Hitchcock's influential Psycho (1960), the sight of a demonically possessed little girl strapped to her bed in William Friedkin's The Exorcist (1973), or the blood gushing silently from the elevator in Stanley Kubrick's masterpiece, The Shining (1980). Add to that list the black and white footage of a quiet graveyard as a car comes driving down its winding pathways, with spiky, sharp stock music like a warning of terror on to its soundtrack. These are the opening images and sounds of George A Romero's horror classic Night of the Living Dead, released all the way back in 1968.

Night of the Living Dead didn't immediately become a hit, and it took years for it to enter the classic film canon. It was an ultra low budget shocker, made on a shoe string budget by a group of friends, some of whom happened to have a bit of experience filming commercials. The fact that Night of the Living Dead still appeals to audiences all over the world really is quite remarkable. The great zombie revival of the past decade or so has seen zom-coms like Simon Pegg and Edgar Wright's Shaun of the Dead (2004), Romero's own return with three more Dead movies (Land of the Dead, Diary of the Dead and Survival of the Dead), remakes of his old classics (Day of the Dead and Dawn of the Dead), a reimagining or two of Night of the Living Dead itself, plus zombie comics, zombie costumes, zombie conventions and the hit TV series Walking Dead, one of the most popular shows of all time, no less. It all comes from this one movie.

That may sound like an overstatement, but it's true. Night of the Living Dead started off the world's fascination with zombies, even if Romero didn't use the Z word specifically. Sure there had been zombies before, but not flesh eaters who seemed to exist only to devour on your loved ones.

But does being so closely attached to the zombie genre haunt Romero? He was asked this very question by the Horror Movies website. "Of course it haunts you," he replied, "I'd love to be able to go in and pitch another kind of film and be taken seriously, but I'm generally not taken seriously. If I were to walk in there with a little romantic comedy, they'd say, What? So that's a bit frustrating because you don't grow up wanting to be a horror filmmaker. You grow up wanting to be a filmmaker and I wish I had a wider range. And I tried early on to do several films that were not genre and nine people saw them, so I don't have the credentials in that regard. There's a bit of frustration there but on the other side of that coin, and far outweighing it is the fact that I've been able to use genre fantasy horror... express my opinion, talk a little bit about society, do a little bit of satire and that's been great, man. A lot of people don't have that platform. So I don't know. I joke and say maybe I'm the Michael Moore of horror but it's wonderful to have that ability. It's sort of my niche. I can go in and do what I want to do."

And of course, any fan of Romero knows there is a lot more to him than just the zombie movies. Even if they do continue to define him, and the fact that he can be seen as the one man responsible for a huge chunk of today's defining pop culture, Romero's quirky filmography as a whole should be praised for the innovative body of work it is. Sure, we have the six "Dead" movies, but also consider his dark vampire-psycho masterpiece Martin, the doomy dread of The Crazies, the very of its time (early 70s) There's Always Vanilla, the truly whacky Creepshow, the disturbing Bruiser and imaginative Money Shines. There is all this and more besides.

In this book I look at each entry in his varied, rich and wonderful filmography. From the primitive fright of Night of the Living Dead, through the mixed horror and drama directorial pieces, the quirky screenplays and most recent Dead flicks, this is a man who deserves his reputation as one of horror's most important directors. Also included are Q and As I have done with various collaborators, who share their memories of this truly wonderful filmmaker.

THE MOVIES

NIGHT OF THE LIVING DEAD (1968)

The 1960s brought in a new golden age for horror in mainstream cinema. Not since the 1930s when Boris Karloff and Bela Lugosi crept around in the shadows with sinister stances had the genre seen such lucrative and thrilling heights. In the UK, film studio Hammer Productions regularly unleashed, what were at the time, genuinely scary and entertaining horror movies. They packed theatres and made big business; cloaked vampires, wild werewolves in torn rags and disrobing beauties provided visual excitement but little else in means of intellectual depths. Not that there was anything wrong with that of course.

But in 1968 the genre was to be redefined in a very dark, angry, gory, bleak and ugly fashion, totally at odds with the glamour and extravagance of the horror of that era. The horror was to reflect the nightmarish goings on in a crumbling world, a world much more terrifying than anything you could put on the screen and dress up as scary. The clichéd gloomy baroque castle was to be replaced by a creaky old farm house in the middle of the woods. Those semi nude babes and caped neck biters were nowhere to be seen in a land of repulsive flesh nibbling monsters, unstoppable in their quest for the blood of the living. The film that changed it all was a low budget black and white picture that came from North of Pittsburgh, USA, called Night of the Living Dead.

However, the very idea of these beings and the term zombie itself originated long before cinema was invented. The term "zombie" was apparently first used in the 1929 book The Magic Island by William Seabrook, although it was spelled Zombi at the time. The black and white 1932 Bela Lugosi film White Zombie had the horror icon ruling over a gang of the undead, and another early cinematic zombie was featured in Ed Wood's appallingly brilliant Plan 9 from Outer Space; but it wasn't particularly scary nor flesh hungry! The zombie apocalypse, what it would become known as, was only around the corner.

George A Romero, a New Yorker who had graduated from Pittsburgh's Carnegie Mellon University, never thought a career in movies was a possibility, but had always dreamt of making a living out of film making. Born in 1940 to a Cuban father and Lithuanian-American mother, the young George found much enjoyment in the ludicrous gore of the old classic EC comics, which would delight him as a young boy and serve to influence his future career as the King of the Gruesome. "I grew up on the old EC Comics, before the Comic

Code," Romero told Blogamole. "I thought they were tremendously moral, and then they got shut down for being immoral... somebody missed the mark there. They were blamed for being too gory. I just loved that stuff."

A film that really captured his young imagination was Tales of Hoffman, which Romero loved. He has cited the film as a big influence, and noted that the special effects in the film, although inspiring, were pretty clear and easy to figure out. "If they can do it, maybe I can," he observed. He had also been to see the old classic horror films, such as Dracula and Frankenstein, on the big screen when they were rereleased in the early fifties. These movies also proved to be very influential to him in his formative years.

George always had the ambition to break into the film world, but like so many other future innovators, he had to start somewhere. In his case it was at the bottom. His first job in the media area was cycling news reels back and forth to editing rooms and gluing them together in the suite. One of Romero's other early jobs for the screen was working on the kid's show Mister Rogers Neighbourhood. Mister Rogers was a children's entertainer and songwriter, with one of the most popular kid's shows of the day. "He gave a lot of people their breaks," he said. "Michael Keaton was a grip when I was working there. Everyone from Pittsburgh started with him."

In the mid 1960s, Romero began directing commercials under the company Latent Image, which he had formed with some of his friends. They also shot industrial shorts and documentaries. During the making of one short film, George found himself filming a tonsillectomy. He enjoyed the experience so much that he planned to make a film which utilized his fondness for filming the graphic imagery of blood and guts more thoroughly. Combining this, and his love of the violent comic books he had read in his youth, Romero got together a new and very interesting idea. He had previously been working with John Russo and Russell Streiner in the company, which by the late 60s had been had been successfully running for years. But with his darker and more daring ambitions taking over, Romero eventually somehow persuaded them to form Ten Productions, a

company with an aim to make their first feature horror film.

It was originally planned that the film would be made for $6,000 with each member of the company putting up $600 each. In the end the budget was raised to an eventual $114,000 thanks to outside funding, when the film was seeing its early stages under various dodgy working titles, such as Monster Flick, Night of Anubis and Night of the Flesh Eaters. At one stage, the script, penned by Romero and John A Russo, was to be centered on a group of teenage aliens.

Romero has since admitted that the original genesis of the film was a short story he had written alone, clearly lifting ideas, or as he puts it "ripping off" Richard Matheson's classic novel I Am Legend.

"I ripped off the siege and the central idea," he said of the film's similarities to Matheson's creation. "Which I thought was so powerful, that this particular plague involved the entire planet. I also felt that, rather than opening with a fait accompli, as in the book, it might be more interesting to observe the world during its collapse, to watch the disintegration of the old guard as its downfall is brought about. But I didn't want to do vampires because he had already done vampires. So what could I do to make it my own? I made them flesh-eaters instead of blood-drinkers. But I never thought of them as zombies; I never called them zombies in Night.... They were 'ghouls' or 'those things.' But it was never really about them. They were just the problem driving the characters; it could have been anything, like a Hitchcock MacGuffin."

Brother and Sister Barbra (Judith O'Dea) and Johnny (Russell Streiner) are visiting a Pennsylvania graveyard upon instructions from their mother, to decorate and take some new flowers to their father's grave. Before too long, five minutes into the film in fact, a strange, pale man wanders his way into the graveyard and attacks Johnny, knocking his head on a grave stone, killing him instantly. In horror Barbra escapes from the man and eventually ends up at an old farm house, where she finds herself teamed with Ben (Duane Jones). As the zombies surround the farm house, they find themselves barricaded inside, along with a couple and their daughter, who has been bitten by one of the creatures. The following 90 minutes are grueling, unpleasant, frightening, intense, occasionally gruesome, overpoweringly claustrophobic and in the end, ultimately tragic. After surviving the ordeal, the next morning, Ben awakes as a group of armed locals arrive to wipe out the zombies. Ben goes to the window and is shot dead by one of the gang, before his body is thrown on to a bonfire alongside stacks and stacks of burning zombies, bodies they have recently destroyed. So much for a happy ending.

While the film was being made, the cast and crew would go out to the cottage for three days and shoot some scenes. Seeing as they would have to sleep at the house, and the fact it had no running water or electricity, they would have to wash in the stream around the back of the cottage. When the three days were up, the crew would return to make a commercial under the Latent Image name, before going back again to shoot more of the movie. This process took months. Romero noted that they were in fact very lucky that the cast stuck with them for so long for very little money.

Russell Streiner's brother Gary had also been one of the ten primary investors and had a notable role in getting the film made. His first job on the picture however, sounds far from glamorous. "George was a chronic soda drinker, and he just couldn't speak in the morning without a cigarette and a Mountain Dew," he said. "Because George was a chain smoker, he put all of his cigarettes out in the bottles. So my first professional job was to get all the cigarette butts out of the pop bottles, so I could then take them up the street and return them for the 3 cent deposit, for my pay check. To kind of get an idea of how many pop bottles there were, there were weeks when I made $50."

He also remembered sitting on the floor watching Romero and co. brainstorm their ideas together in the Pittsburgh Latent Image building, feeling out of his depth with the intellectuals, or the "big boys" as he put it. It seems that even at such an early stage in his directorial film career, Romero was full of interesting ideas, the "leader" so to speak from the word go, but not in a dictatorial way. George is the chilled out guy who just happens to have the final say.

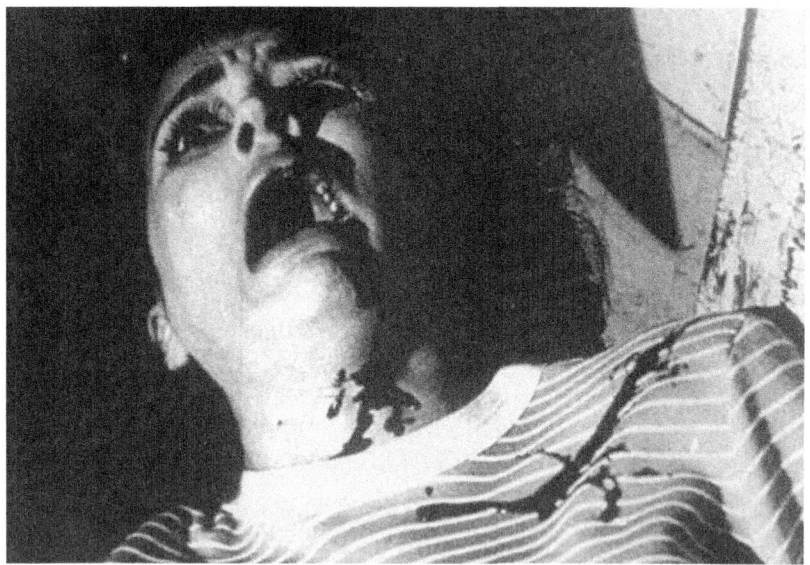

Due to the lack of a proper film budget, most of the production and acting was done by members of Ten Productions and their friends. The special effects didn't come too expensive either; the blood used in the film was chocolate syrup, while the flesh and guts which the zombies chewed on was ham and entrails brought to the set by one of the cast, who also happened to be a butcher. Camera work was also done by the team, while Karl Hardman, another Ten Productions member, took the role of shooting and developing film stills. The small budget is not apparent when watching the film over 40 years later though and the cheap 35mm black and white film Romero used only enhances the eeriness. The blackness makes it one of the creepiest and most unsettling films ever made. In its primitive simplicity, is has taken on a raw, gothic feel which sends shivers down the spine.

Visuals aside, much of the mystery of the movie is what makes it the all the more scary. For instance, there is never a real explanation given to the fact that the dead seem to have just come back to life and have begun eating the living. But as in all the Romero films, various characters have different takes and theories as to why the creatures are roaming the land, and we the viewer perhaps are open and free enough, during the duration of the film, to make up our own minds.

"When we originally shot the Night of the Living Dead thing, there were three proposed causes," said Romero. "…and we cut two of them out because the scenes were boring and the scenes around them were boring, and that one we left in because it was part of that newscast and it made it seem a little bigger. And that became for a while, people said, 'Oh, that's what happened.' You know, some Venus probe came back and brought some kind of bug. I don't want there to be a cause, it's just something that's happening, it's just a different deal, it's a different way of life. If you want to look at it as a revolution, a new society coming in and devouring the old, however you want to look at it. That's really my take on it, it doesn't matter. And, people just don't communicate to get to the core of it at all, they just have their own agendas or their own concerns.."

Romero never called the creatures in the film 'zombies' and didn't have any of the characters utter the word either. Obviously to him and the viewers alike, especially 40 odd years on, the use of that particular word would sound corny in the disturbing, at times realistic content. Not only that, the term "zombie" is limiting. There are many options for a Romero fan to consider. To Romero himself though, zombies "were voodoo boys in the Caribbean doing the wet work for Bela Lugosi." It wasn't until critics began to refer to the creatures in Night of the Living Dead as zombies, that the film found itself associated with the creatures and as a result, became the key representative of the genre.

Night of the Living Dead premiered in October 1968 at Fulton Theatre in Pittsburgh. As the film was unrated, people all of all ages, mostly children, decided to buy tickets and check out this new horror movie that had come to town. Horror films up to that point could be enjoyed by everyone, as there was never a large amount of gore and they were generally camp affairs on the whole. But the reaction that night to Romero's zombie thriller was, to put it lightly, extreme. Critic Roger Ebert commented that the "kids" were terrified! He went on with: "The movie had stopped being delightfully scary about halfway through, and had become unexpectedly terrifying. There was a little girl across the aisle from me, maybe nine years old, who was sitting very still in her seat and crying. I don't think the younger kids really knew what hit them. They were used to going to movies, sure, and they'd seen some horror movies before, sure, but this was something else. This was ghouls eating people up, and you could actually see what they were eating. This was little girls killing their mothers. This was being set on fire. Worst of all, even the hero got killed."

The film was not an instant commercial success on a huge scale, but at least made its money back fairly quickly. It also proved to be popular in drive-in theatres. At first, as is the case with all horror movies, it garnered very little serious criticism. When a number of months passed however, critics began to pick up on the fact that there was a little more to the horror on display than met the eye. Romero was certainly saying a few things about American culture and the film spoke to a generation that was disillusioned with the lost ideals of peace and love and painfully destroyed by the pointless bloodshed of the Vietnam War. There was also the fear in the 1960s, that nuclear fall out could result in mass radiation and disease. The film reeked of pale fear.

Night of the Living Dead though was firstly picked up in the French press as "essential American cinema," much to the surprise of Romero and all involved. "It stunned all of us," Romero claimed. It was also later invited into the Museum of Modern Art.

Interest in the film soon grew to a level that it was packing out theatres, shocking some and bringing perverse joy to others. For its time, Night of the Living Dead was very gory, unprecedented in its often grotesque visuals and as dark as cinema could get. But considering this, the film costing little over 100, 000 still managed to make back 42 million dollars at the box office!

Critics treated the film, in most part, as a dangerous and grotesque piece of work. The New York Times for instance called it "junk" while others such as Variety hated the gore, calling it "an orgy of sadism." The celebrated film critic Pauline Kael though, was more complimentary. She claimed it was "one of the most gruesomely terrifying movies ever made!" And Rex Reed was encouraging too. "If you want to see what turns a B movie into a classic, don't miss Night of the Living Dead," he wrote. "It is unthinkable for anyone seriously interested in horror movies not to see it." Joseph Madley, a film historian, called it "a documentary on the loss of social stability."

Seeing as Romero was influenced in his formative years by wild, uncensored comic books (one of his favourite moments in one of the EC comics involved a baseball player's heart being ripped out and used as third base), one can see that the director definitely adapted the simplicity of the page on to the big screen. Every Romero shot, whether it be in an action or non action sequence, contains a definite clearness. There are no shoddy shot set ups and everyone and everything is always clearly defined on the screen before your eyes.

There is meticulous care given to each image and there is also much detail within the shot itself. In this film, and especially in Dawn of the Dead, you tend to notice things on the tenth viewing (if you've watched them that many times of course) that you maybe didn't spot on the first or second. But the strength of his ability to provide us with strong imagery, the covering his ass as he puts it, is what gives his movies a true depth.

Although the media, when looking back on key pieces of art from the past, like to add neat little connotations to fit with their view of the times, Night of the Living Dead does contain some seemingly naïve and revolutionary anger. For Romero and countless others like him, peace and love had failed in its quest for harmony and if anything, things were only getting worse in the world. The Vietnam War was in full swing, in all its horror and as a result Romero's view on mankind was that it was "disintegrating". The Village Voice summed up the underlying themes when Elliot Stein wrote, "the zombie carnage seemed a grotesque echo of the conflict raging in Vietnam."

The climax of the film, far from a feel good ending, was possibly the most disturbing part of it. The fact that the hero has made it through the violence, survived the duration of the horrifying picture, and then is killed carelessly by a posse of gun toting loons was, especially at the time, very hard to swallow. Leaving the theatre with a smile was always what the viewer ideally wanted, yet Romero had left them all on a downer, when in truth, their life outside the theatre was far from rosy in the first place. Family members may not have returned from war, and if they had they may have gone mad with what they'd seen over there. Things were not living up to their supposed potential and the American Dream seemed shattered. Only a year later, Dennis Hopper and Peter Fonda would perhaps more clearly and intentionally define this saddened era with the angry Easy Rider.

While Romero made the creatures in Night of the Living Dead bad in a ghoulish, inhumane, relentless and almost animal like way, he made the humans who come in near the final reel (the news crews and the armed posse) the worst of all. Perhaps he was pointing out the fact that man himself is his own worst enemy. This is a recurring theme in all of the Romero zombie films.

While a lot has been said about the points Romero was making with Night of the Living Dead, he told the AV Club he is not a man that offers any conclusions to the problems put forward in his films. He also noted that much of the power in the film's subtext, no matter how intriguing and provocative it may be, is more likely to be a result of accident and coincidence. "You know what," Romero said. "I'm not trying to preach, or ask questions. Well, maybe *ask* questions, but certainly not answer any questions. I'm really trying to shoot snapshots. I made the first film, then all of a sudden people started to write about it like it was an essential American movie. And a lot of that was accidental. We cast an African-American actor because he was the best actor from among our friends. There's a certain anger in the movie already, but a lot of why that film gets applause is because Wayne is a black guy. In the script, his race is never mentioned. In

my mind, when I wrote that initial scene, he was a white guy. And he would've been shot by the police even if he *was* a white guy. But because he happened to be an African-American, that made it much stronger, particularly after the assassination. We shouldn't take all the credit for that. A lot of it was an accident."

When shooting on the film had been completed, Romero had driven the finished product to New York so he could show it to the investors. It was on the way there when he heard the news on the radio that Martin Luther King had been shot dead. "That made it stronger again," he said. "It was unintentional. I can't take any credit for that."

It is true that at the time, using a black actor like Duane Jones as the lead character was a rather new idea for cinema. In the original script, the character was to be a white truck driver of "low intelligence." Romero has stated that Jones refused to play the role in the way it was written and so took charge of his part, putting a new, stronger slant on it. Romero also recalled that Duane was concerned about the possible consequences of having a black lead doing the things he was doing in this picture. "I'm the guy whose got to go out in the street after slugging this white dame," he said. Once again, Romero had over looked any potential outrage. When Duane brought up the fact that this was ahead of its time, Romero would say "come on man its 1968, we're past all that." However, even *he* would eventually begin to realise the strength in such an unusual casting decision. It has to be said that the unpleasant ending, when Ben gets through hell and is killed anyway by the heartless posse, reminds one sourly of the grotesque lynching of black men in the South of America many moons ago.

The role of Barbra, played by Judith O'Dea, was primarily written as a "strong" character, but Romero and Russo changed their script when they saw O'Dea's almost catatonic portrayal of the woman. She totally captures the true terror of being in such a horrifying situation, unusually realistic for a horror film, especially one made in 1968. As a result however, feminists took issue with all the female characters in Night of the Living Dead, particularly Barbra, who they thought did nothing for female power at all. Of course, Romero had nothing like this in mind either when he began directing the film.

Romero's relaxed attitude, both on set and in person is to those who have worked with him, one of his most endearing qualities, along with his modesty. But accident, fluke or whatever one might dress it as, Night of the Living Dead changed and redefined the horror genre. He was the first filmmaker who dressed down the horror genre, in as much as he made people accept that the locations could be mundane, ordinary places. There didn't have to be extravagant sets at all. In fact, the idea of hell unfolding in your street or in the woods near your house, made it all the more frightening. The film is also a precursor to the more violent and gory horror flicks to follow, including the much criticised, but also much loved "Slasher" movie, as well as the exploitation thrillers and the slew of zombie flicks that followed in the same vein as Night of the Living Dead. Speaking of its influence and popularity all these years on, Romero told Rick Curnutte that he never expected such a reaction: "You know, we didn't know that it would ever get recognized. I mean, we took it seriously. We really were trying to make it as much a metaphor as it was a thrill ride. And I've always tried... I don't know, I've never wanted to just do movies about guys in hockey masks with knives, you know? I don't think that way. I sort of think of what underlies it first."

After the film was released, George and Russo made an agreement to go their separate ways and allowed each other to do what they wanted. Eventually, Russo created the Return of the Living Dead series (inventing the myth that zombies crave "Braaaaiiiinnnsss!") and Romero, at first, left the zombie genre for more varied areas.

AN INTERVIEW WITH JUDITH O'DEA
(BARBRA IN NIGHT OF THE LIVING DEAD)

When did you first meet Romero?

I believe the first time George and I met was at an audition for another feature film he wanted to make. This must have been at least three years prior to my Night audition. He nor his work was familiar to me at the time, so I can't really share any thoughts with you about that.

Did you think at the time that the film was kind of breaking some ground with a black lead and a strong female character?

To be honest with you, Chris, I really didn't go so far as to think we were being ground breaking. I saw Duane Jones as another actor not a 'black' actor. Being in a feature film was just so exciting for me that that was where my thoughts were focused. I just wanted to do the best job... the most believable job I could for George and company.

What was atmosphere like on the set? People say Romero flicks are like a big family.

The hours were long, but we didn't care. I can't say I felt we were an extended family during the shoot, but we certainly tried our best to work together well in order to make the best film possible with minimal resources.

At the time did you think you were just making any old horror film or did you see it as a special piece that might endure?

I had no idea we were making a film that would endure as long as it has. The project was a job, something I was thrilled to be a part of; my first feature film! That it has done as well as it has over the years is pure 'icing on the cake' for all of us.

What is the line or moment people most recall of you in the film?

The line most recalled about me in the film is not something I said, but what my brother Johnny (Russell Streiner) said to me..."They're coming to get you, Barbra!" It is not so much strange as it is amazing, humbling, and honestly, forever thrilling, Chris.

THERE'S ALWAYS VANILLA (1971)

"I don't think of it as a complete film..."
- *Romero on There's Always Vanilla*

Definitely Romero's most buried, forgotten and overlooked movie has to be 1971's There's Always Vanilla. As an artistic follow up to the seminal horror classic Night of the Living Dead, romantic comedy fare such as this was certainly brave and admirable, although destined to be career suicide. But Romero wasn't a man interested in a bog standard career, and even by his second feature, he was worried of becoming type cast. He once said that as a kid he had wanted to be a filmmaker (a pipe dream as he called it), and not strictly a horror filmmaker. Like the great legendary directors who emerged around the same time as him - Coppola and Scorsese for instance - Romero wasn't just interested in scaring his audience, he also wanted to make them think, sit up and challenge the status quo. Unfortunately, with Night of the Living Dead being such a strong and powerful statement on the decay of society, he was immediately held up as THE American horror master, and as a result, nobody was interested in seeing a film like There's Always Vanilla; which, of course, is a shame, as it isn't that bad and is well worth a look for both Romero addicts and fans of early 70s cinema.

"Our title was There's Always Vanilla," Romero said in an interview, "and they changed it to The Affair. It never got a good distribution. It opened in a few theatres and never caught on. It was a small distributor who didn't have the clout to circulate film. I don't know if the film would ever have been a big success on any level, but this guy just opened it in a few theatres and just folded his hands. I mean, he never even tried."

From the opening reels though, the film is inventive, engrossing and appealing. Romero's thorough directorial style establishes an immediate mood of curiosity, so that from the first minute or so, you can tell you will be hooked on this strange little picture. Even though it wasn't written by Romero (that credit goes to Rudy Rucci, as the film was intended to merely showcase the acting of Raymond Laine), it still possesses his all important "cover your ass" shooting style and sense of humour.

The film follows Chris Bradley (Laine), an ex solider who submits to his father's family business and heads home to Pittsburgh to step up to the plate. He moves in with attractive model Lynn (Judith Ridley from Night of the Living Dead). who begins to realise she has to carry the lazy and irresponsible Chris. While she ponders whether or not to abort their baby, he gets a proper job at an ad firm, a post he soon quits. Eventually she leaves him, and Chris moves in with his old man.

The film is nothing spectacular, anyone would admit that, but judging by Romero's own chosen words about the picture, you would surely have been expecting much worse than this. So I was pleasantly surprised when I realised that I had actually enjoyed the film as a whole. The performances are good and quite believable, and the film has a definite warmth and charm to it. However, it was this film that led to Romero parting creative ways with his Night of the Living Dead collaborators, John Russo and Russell Streiner, although he proclaimed that they stayed friends.

"It wasn't my script," Romero said in one interview. "I just think the film was a little frothy. It wasn't accomplished enough for my taste. I have no objection to anyone seeing it. But I didn't think it would be worth anyone's while to watch it. I don't mind it being available. I don't think it's bad. I don't think it's terribly well made considering the money we had. Very loose... didn't really explore what it's meant to explore."

Vanilla is typical of its era, a post-Graduate, post-Summer of Love exploration of bohemian ideals, exposing the harshness of reality where work commitment and responsibility must out rule reckless freedom. He had projected rebellion with Night of the Living Dead, and captured late 1960s anger. With There's Always Vanilla, he quietly reflected the lost, aimless feel of the early 70s. As a result though, the film itself often feels lost and aimless, never really too sure of itself as a story or a proper statement. Still, this isn't as bad as Romero makes it out to be. There's no horror and definitely no zombies, but enough good things here to please a Romero admirer.

SEASON OF THE WITCH (1973)

In the supposed "lost era" of Romero's career, in between the releases of Night of the Living Dead and Dawn of the Dead, the man most know as the King of the Zombies made some pretty interesting films to say the least. These movies were varied, colourful, bold and daring, and unfortunately none of them have got even half of the credit they deserve. Season of the Witch was another low budget flick, this one released in 1973, and it's also gone out under the titles Hungry Wives and Jack's Wife. Season of the Witch though, you have to admit, is a much more eye catching title.

"There's Always Vanilla and Jack's Wife were seen by very few people," Romero said in one recent interview, "and I am not sure what my fans today would make of them. Maybe they'll see a little bit of my style, maybe they'll see a little bit of my head in there. There is always something instinctive. You can look at an artist's work and you can maybe see a little something there."

Romero had a point. Season of the Witch (the title I am going to refer to this film by) may not seem totally typical a subject matter for Romero, our zombie godfather, but there is much more to him than the stumbling undead. He is a masterful director in the truest sense and his movies are never thrown together in the slightest. If you compare his Dead movies to straight to video or B movie zombie flicks of the 80s and 90s, the comparisons are non existent. He never liked zombies for zombies sake, they were always a tool for metaphors and subtext. But when you think of the camera angles, the way he gets you inside the story, in the depth of the characters' desperate situations, he is a few miles above even the most notable horror filmmakers. He establishes a mood of fear, dread and utter hopelessness, but never gets us too bogged down in the negative aspects of the dichotomies the characters are stuck in. He may use gore, but never as the premier attraction. It's usually as a way to remind you that the fear the characters are feeling is justified and they are very much in danger.

But Season of the Witch definitely stands alone in his filmography, although stylistically it is very much a Romero movie. The direction brings to mind some of the most chilling moments of Night of the Living Dead, so even a complete zombie junkie will find something to take away from a picture such as this.

What hinders the wide discovery of this film was its messy release. Filmed as Jack's Wife, Romero and his small reliable crew were intent on shooting a proper study of the realm of the occult with their tiny $100,000 budget. However, the film's distributor got busy with the film reels, cutting out integral scenes and putting it out into the world as a kind of soft core porno flick under the title Hungry Wives.

It went out in 1973 to a mostly muted response. In fact it wasn't until he made good with Dawn of the Dead in 1978 that the film was rereleased and of course reappraised under its new title Season of the Witch. With such a muddled past, perhaps one can see why Romero never fully accepts it as a proper part of his filmography.

The film takes place in Pittsburgh, where bored wife Joan Mitchell (played by Jan White) gets tired of her violent, sexist husband's ways. As she and her friends discover a new mysterious addition to the neighbourhood, Marion (Virginia Greenwald), Joan begins to learn about witchcraft. After a tarot reading, it is revealed that Marion is the leader of a witches' coven. When Joan grows even lonelier and more frustrated, she obtains a book about witchcraft. She puts a spell on the man who is seeing her daughter, Gregg (Raymond Laine again), so that he becomes attracted to her. In between this, Joan has consistently horrific nightmares and in the end, kills her husband, before joining Marion's coven.

As straight forward horror, Season of the Witch is not exactly frightening. Instead, it deals with the occult in a more literal and intelligent way, and is never over the top nor totally unbelievable. Where the movie is perhaps more interesting is in its underlying subtext. Clearly, Romero is using the witches coven as a symbolic manifestation of the women's movement, the witches being feminists rising up against their sexist and dominating males. Romero using feminism in film is nothing radical for him though; in many ways he was one of the first forward thinking, radical, casually feminist directors in the horror genre, or any genre for that matter.

Romero's feminist leanings didn't begin right away in his first film though, at least not by his own choice. Like his openness to casting black lead actors, his knack of writing strong female characters developed over time. In Night of the Living Dead, Barbra is little more than a catatonic cardboard cut out, as much a zombie as the creeping flesh eaters outside the barn. She's the quintessential horror film chick, running and screaming from the creatures, then being no use to herself or anyone through most of the picture. Gaylen Ross's character in Dawn of the Dead however, as pregnant and morning sick as she is throughout, is not a screamer, nor a hopeless fleer of the dead. Even if it's only due to the fact that Gaylen refused to scream as the script wished her to, she was a step towards Sigourney Weaver in Alien territory. Season of the Witch then, put out before Dawn to little fan fair, was more direct in its revolutionary approach, how conscious or unconscious it all was.

The AV Club saw it as a long lost cousin to Ang Lee's acclaimed movie The Ice Storm, in as much that both films, in very different ways, reflect a changing time in early 70s suburbia, exploring the forbidden and the mysterious goings on in what appears to be the average neighbourhood. I would liken it to the 1985 Madonna hit Desperately Seeking Susan, which of course seems to be a very odd comparison on the surface. Yet in that film, Rosanna Arquette plays an upper middle class housewife, bored of her marriage to a wealthy business man. Her friends might envy her for all the shallow materialism of her life, but she is trapped and seeks escapism. Whereas Arquette's character chooses to follow the exotic life of wild child Susan (Madonna), whose adventures she follows in the local paper, Joan Mitchell the hungry wife turns to the liberating power of witchcraft. So is this horror? Is this a film of witchcraft and the occult? Yes and no. Again, Romero is simply using the horror template to explore something with more depth. Whereas he seemed a little lost in the midst of There's Always Vanilla - a film much closer to Brian De Palma's early New York art house pictures (Hi Mom and Greetings, both starring a young Robert De Niro) than anything Romeroesque - Season of the Witch *feels* like a Romero film, and he is very much in his own territory.

Although the original cut is not in existence (despite the odd deleted scene popping up here and there), the currently available version of the film is the closest we will get to Romero's vision. There are some undeniably good scenes, up there with George's finest cinematic stand outs. The mood he sets in the scene when Joan hears her daughter having an orgasm during the storm is utterly uncomfortable and powerful, especially when you consider the fact she is actually semi-masturbating to the sound of her daughter making love. But it's the shadows that cast and the imposing statues in close up which make the scene truly unforgettable. She is the ultimate bored housewife, reduced to getting off on her own daughter getting *her* rocks off. Again, as in Night of the Living Dead, Romero blows apart the established standard dynamic of the family household; disturbing and delighting in equal measure.

"There's only one that *I* would like to remake which is actually the third film that I made, called Season of the Witch," Romero told Cinema Blend, "and I didn't have enough money to do it well and I think that I could really do a good job with it today. I've sort of been noodling on an updated script for it, but it's the only one that I would even think about remaking. Most of my stuff was sort of of-the-time."

AN INTERVIEW WITH
JOEDDA McCLAIN
(STAR OF SEASON OF THE WITCH)

How did you end up getting the part in Romero's Season of the Witch?

I was 21, working as a model , doing commercials and voice over work in Pittsburgh. Pa. My agent told me about the casting call. There were a lot of girls ,I was shocked when I got the part. At that point in George's career Living Dead was not a cult film yet. He was not being viewed as a serious filmmaker. When I first met him I thought he was very cool , and funny. At the interview there was a lot of joking and banter.

Do you remember the first day on set?

I was a nervous wreck the 1st day. The 2 leads were N Y actors. I was very anxious about my inexperience. Everyone was very professional . That was a crazy time, I expected to have some confrontations about sexual advances That was pretty standard at the time. Nothing like that happened. It was a FIRST!! I was really happy working with the whole cast.

What was he like to work with?

George definitely had a vision; he could see the film in his mind. We worked long days, he was very interesting and present.

Did you like the film when you saw it?

I was definitely disappointed with the finished product. I think George wanted the film to be dark , a twisted look at current lifestyles. A lot was left on the cutting room floor. I doubt any of us felt it looked like we were expecting. It was altogether a time of growth and expansion for me. I was very grateful for the opportunity. I never saw George again after the screening party. When his career became such a cult following, I was happy to say I worked with him.

THE CRAZIES (1973)

Just as Night of the Living Dead defined the modern zombie movie and started off decades of imitations and reimaginings of the slow moving undead scenario, The Crazies singlehandedly invented the highly popular panicky apocalyptic pandemic movie. Without The Crazies, there'd be none of those high paced fright fests consisting of fast moving, foamy mouthed infected fiends out to feast upon you and tear you limb from limb. In a world without The Crazies, there's no Rabid, no Shivers, no 28 Days Later, no Cabin Fever; the list goes on. But while Night of the Living Dead's mighty influence is voiced time and again in both horror and mainstream circles, widely recognised by even the most casual of horror fans as the singular daddy of the zombie flick, The Crazies' appeal is more cult, underground, and as Romero himself would say, trollish. It might have made only a small dint of impact at the time of its release, but The Crazies is another one of Romero's terrifying, traumatic gems which has lasted through time and remains a classic after all these decades.

"It's amazing that my films have such a shelf life," George told Electric Sheep Magazine. "When I go to these conventions – horror conventions and so forth – there are fans of all of the films, and that's really great. I love talking about them with people, people who are discovering films that no one went to see in the first place. I don't know about The Crazies. It has its fans – people who really like it a lot – but I don't know about its legacy. Certainly the remake, that was a zombie movie, but I never thought of it that way. Thematically, I was sort of doing the same thing with The Crazies as Night – people responding to a situation, except there I made them mad!"

In many ways, The Crazies could actually be seen as his most direct and believable exercise in terrorising the audience, and is perhaps a more honest approach to true horror than any of the Dead films. Zombies themselves, these days at least, have almost become parodies of themselves, watered down so much through mainstream money making culture that they no longer send a shiver of genuine dread down the spine, but a warm glow of familiarity. Those flesh eating creeps from Night of the Living Dead were utterly frightening, ghoulish and scary reflections of all of us; a revolution from the inside, the new eating the old. However, when Romero made Dawn of the Dead, he turned them into comic book zombies, or the most part at least (more of that later). While he re-established that doom in the chilling and wonderful Day of the Dead, zombies were then adopted for the masses, mutated into the world of unlikely major front page pop culture.

Check out Michael Jackson's Thriller for example, the lighter Return of the Living Dead movies and so forth. Now, Zombies are ideal Halloween costume fodder for ten year olds. So while Romero's instalments remain terrifying, he is no longer "the only kid in the playground" as he once put it. And the most popular of them all is The Walking Dead, which is not that scary; it is great at times, but definitely not scary. (Romero called it a soap opera with zombies.) The Crazies however is more real and jagged, with the plausible idea that people may get infected and go, in a word, nuts. In an age when increasingly cruel methods of warfare and their vile capabilities are seen every day, and with the threat of social meltdown looming over us at all times, a break out on the scale of the one in The Crazies is not so much a horrific nightmare, but more like putting on the ten o'clock news. His direction was definitely newsy and done in a gritty documentary style in Night of the Living Dead, but in The Crazies it's even more urgent, frantic and disturbing.

The film follows the premise of a plane crashing in Pennsylvania, releasing a mysterious virus which gets into the water supply (Cabin Fever anyone?) and begins to turn the town's folk utterly mad and homicidal in their urges. Back in the early 70s, what with the Cold War and Vietnam still very much clogging up the air, The Crazies must have been a distressing film to watch. But now, a time where we are constantly on our toes waiting for the next horrifying news items of bloody terrorism and mass hysteria, it's hardly a pleasant watch. It's bleak, claustrophobic, and totally plausible too.

The scariest part of The Crazies though is when we witness the gruesome and unsettling effects this bio-weapon has on our heroes. For me the most interesting and strange relationship in the film is between Artie (played by the great Richard Liberty) and his daughter Kathie (the equally great Lynn Lowry). He's the doting, protective father who, when the madness takes him, feels an incestuous desire for his daughter, who he believes to be his dead wife. Again, as in Night of the Living Dead and Season of the Witch, Romero rips the all American family in two.

In order to understand The Crazies as a stand alone film though, not merely viewing it as one of his inferior movies in the wake of Night of the Living Dead - films which some feel would have been completely forgotten had he not had his name attached to them - we need to cast ourselves back to 1973. George was now split from his Latent Image pals, out there alone with a new co-worker, producer Alvin Croft. After Night, George had turned down bigger budget Hollywood offers, who as he put it, wanted him to make another "one of these." George of course relented the Hollywood machine and was intent on not becoming typecast as the go-to zombie guy. With two commercial misfires following Night, Romero's career was in a bad way. Proper horror came calling.

With The Crazies, he wasn't revisiting the zombie genre as such, but he was certainly skirting on the edge of it, creating a similar atmosphere of panic and mayhem. Again, the people are just trying to survive and we are side by side with them through their struggles. Originally beginning its life as The Mad People, a script by Paul McCollough, it was producer Lee Hessel who read it and passed it along to George. It was all set to be his next feature, but only under the condition that Romero could rewrite it and focus more on the military overtake of the small town. Romero got his wish, and even though the filming went smoothly, the distribution was almost non existent and the film did poorly indeed. At the time of its release, The Crazies sank without much of a trace, and only in recent years has it seen something of a revival of interest. While a lot of Romero puritans turn their noses up at the high speed 2010 remake, the two are very different beasts and really cannot be compared. Even those not fond of the reimagining must be grateful that its arrival brought more notice and acclaim upon George's original creation.

Modern reviews and blogs seem to pick it out as something of a genre classic, with Oh The Horror writing "The Crazies might feel like a bit of a rehash if one approaches it after exhausting Romero's Dead films; however, taking it chronologically, the film feels like the natural extension of Night, while acting as a prelude for his later works. It would be disingenuous to consider The Crazies to be another Dead film with Crazies substituted for Zombies, precisely because the title characters are even more of a non-entity than the Dead. This, perhaps, is Romero's greatest use of irony, as one must wonder if the term in the title shouldn't apply to everyone by the end of the film."

But the movie has just as many haters as fans. On Bloody Disgusting, the film was torn in half by the writer, who claimed that the film was poor on every level, especially technically. "His best films deserve praise. But his worst films, like The Crazies, deserve to be bashed. A cheapness permeates the entire movie. Case in point — the scene where the priest sets himself on fire. There's an art to every aspect of filmmaking. That includes the art of looking cheap. But the single worst thing about The Crazies is without question the editing. There's a cut like every two seconds. Your eye never has a chance to get interested in what it's seeing. The years Romero spent editing commercials really does him a disservice here."

While I can see the writer's view, I don't find The Crazies to be so badly put together at all. Sure it *is* creaky in parts, but it was low budget and a quarter of a million dollars really wasn't a lot of money in those days to make a film with. Nowadays, with digital techniques and relatively cheap editing costs, one can produce a technically perfect gem on such a budget. But we are talking over 40 years ago here. Besides, under the slightly cheap look is a film masterfully put together by a director of extraordinary capabilities. Romero can establish a mood of helpless dread like no one else, but always holds back enough to keep a space for that all important shred of hope. That said, The Crazies is definitely one of his very darkest pictures; and it's not for the zombie gore, as there isn't any here. It's down to the characters and the way they are portrayed, broad yet still controlled performances within a hectic framework.

Romero consistently delivers unforgettable imagery that is both simplistic and stark, moments of chilling horror that are obvious yet imaginative. In all of The Crazies, the one image which sticks with me the most is when the town is being taken over by the traumatic arrival of the white suited, gas masked military. They enter a home where a little boy is holding a toy gun. His look of terror is burned into my brain (obviously the kid is really terrified in real life too), and the feet of the scurrying military men as they step past the child's toy soldiers is utterly powerful. As Roger Ebert might have said, Romero was one of the few men who gave horror a bit more content and class than it really ever required.

Of course, The Crazies has its more obvious moments of vile horror. The opening scene is one of the darkest scenes in any Romero film, where the father has killed the mother and then proceeds to burn the house down. And who could forget its most notorious scene, the knitting needle killing that it's become famous for.

It's important to remember that the film was made while the Vietnam war was still raging on, when images of naked children with burnt skin, running down endless empty roads were plastered all over the press. It was an angry time, one which Romero reflects sublimely. He had pointed out where we were going wrong with Night in 68, and it seemed that five years on, things were only getting worse. In The Crazies, Romero tells us we are helpless against the establishment and their decisions, no matter how hurriedly they are acted out. It's chilling to think that if they wanted us sealed off, shot, disposed of, or out of the picture all together, they'd be able to achieve that in very little time and have a reasonable explanation for doing so. Despite its obvious technical imperfections then, this is a very important film, the first in a sub-genre that gradually grew out of its low key arrival.

MARTIN (1977)

It may be Romero's favourite of his own movies, but even nearly 40 years on, for me at least, it is also his most disturbing. As Texas Chainsaw Massacre director Tobe Hopper pointed out, it's not the ghouls you should be scared of, but the real people. Martin goes by this rule and from the word go is an uncomfortable, unsettling and fiendish experience. It is also brilliant.

John Amplas delivers a tour de force career best performance as Martin, a young man with vampiric allusions, a fantasist who dreams gothic visions of seduction and isolation, a daydreaming outcast who sees himself as the victim of torch holding mobs in these strange dark fantasies. Not just a day dreaming loner, we also know Martin is dangerous and twisted from the word go. In one of the film's most disturbing scenes, Martin kills a young woman on a night train, injects her with drugs, slits her wrist open and drinks her blood.

The young Martin is taken in by Cuda, his granduncle, where he takes shelter with the old man and his daughter, Martin's cousin. Cuda believes Martin is a full on vampire, warning him off his daughter by using clichéd methods as a threat (garlic, crosses etc.), thus heightening Martin's sense of egomaniacal power. Martin feels victimised, but Cuda's fears are justified.

The clever thing about Martin, like Season of the Witch, is that Romero never really lets us know what is real, fantasy or a product of fear, in this case a deep fear of the vampire. Martin lives like a vamp, but even he admits to his granduncle that "there's no real magic." Romero has never been too interested in supernatural explanations, and in all his Dead movies only really alludes to why the dead are coming back to life. It's all left to the mystery, the imagination, which makes the films age better and not appear silly down the line with dated technological or scientific theories. Martin is very much the same, as it's left to us to decide what Martin really is.

In the end, Martin becomes a tragic figure, feared, hated and inevitably sacrificed. After what he has done throughout the whole movie, why is it that we pity him? Well, it's due to Amplas's multi layered performance, which brings to mind Malcolm McDowell's mischievous portrayal of Alex in A Clockwork Orange. Like Alex, Martin is very much a monster in more ways than one, yet we still feel for him. He's a victim of himself after all, a sufferer of a crippling, life ruling addiction.

"I was cast in a musical in my senior year," Amplas told Terror Trap. "I admit, musicals are not my thing. But apparently I moved well, so there I was. For whatever reason, George Romero came and saw the production. My work in that musical turned out to be my audition.

The legend is that George originally wrote Martin as an older character. After seeing my performance, he went away, rewrote the script... and called me and offered me the role of Martin a few months later. Early that fall, I was in front of the camera."

Interestingly, Amplas also explained that the characters in horror he found most appealing were the tragic ones, those who couldn't help their actions. "All of them are blamed for something they didn't do," he said, "or things about themselves that they can't help. Or they do something out of necessity, to live or protect themselves, not to arbitrarily kill or destroy others. It is those kinds of characters I find appealing to watch. They create a kind of psychological horror."

Although Martin is nowhere near as iconic or remembered as Frankenstein (in particular Boris Karloff's moving portrayal of the Monster), he is a similar figure; more loathsome, granted, but slightly pathetic too despite his murderous, blood dinking ways. Romero once again lifts horror above the simplistic exploitation it so usually dines out on, and gives us a deeper, more symbolic portrait of the vampire. Here, Martin is the long suffering addict, the drug frenzied maniac who will do anything for his fix. Like a heroin junkie, Martin is unstoppable in his quest for blood. This is no glamorous Bela Lugosi charm-fest, there are no gothic castles in sight, and there aren't any attractive young vamps seducing their victims as in the likes of, say, True Blood. Whereas the modem day screen vampire is hedonistic, reckless, and often sexy, Martin is sleazy, dirty and slightly pitiful. He's trapped in a personal hell he doesn't wish to be in, but at the same time relishes. Such is the mystery of Martin.

Although Amplas is great in the film (as are some of the supporting cast), the star of the show, once again, is George A.

Romero, stripping the vampire legend bare and exposing the grit beneath the usual glamorous polish. His camerawork nails the demythologisation sublimely, as does the hard edged, harsh, spiky cinematography. It's a glimpse into the diary of a mad man, and no punches are pulled. There is no attempt to make this enjoyable on a visual level either, save perhaps for the fantasy sequences, which are purposely more appealing and romanticised. These sequences however are more of an escape for Martin than the audience. In all though, it's utterly merciless as an exploration into dark addiction, and the tormented existence of the hopelessly hooked.

Again, Martin didn't make much of an impact back in the day, but is now seen as something of a little horror gem. Wicked Horror recently wrote a piece on the movie, explaining its individuality in Romero's filmography:

"Unlike Night of the Living Dead, this is told through the monster's perspective. But that monster is human. He does terrible things, but he is also the protagonist. Whether or not he is the antagonist is part of the reason why the movie still resonates. Is Martin the true monster of the movie, or is it his uncle? Or society? Like life, there are no easy answers. In this it is similar to the zombie trilogy because nothing is clear-cut and there is a wealth of gray area. Romero is not telling us whether or not we should side with Martin, whether we should feel sorry for him or cheer for his inevitable end, like we do for Dracula. No, the director smartly believes that we can come to our own conclusions about the character and the horrific events that unfold throughout the story. It's a relevant movie because it just feels so effortless and honest in its portrayal of a deeply troubled human being. Even after so many years and so many features in the genre, Romero considers Martin to be his best work and it's easy to see why."

"Martin is a serious, dark, dramatic, and thought-provoking horror film," wrote Oh the Horror. "George A. Romero expertly tells the story of Martin through the use of the film stock, shooting on 16mm, using the locations of the industrial-and-steel stricken and worn out town of Braddock, and the haunting jazz (yes, jazz) score from Donald Rubinstein. Every element of the film, both visual and through audio, creates an atmosphere of dread and haunting loneliness that I'm sure everyone of us has felt."

Personally, I am not so sure I would limit Martin by calling it a horror film at all. It certainly has its moments of horror, but they are more real, gut wrenching and sickening, just as believable as the brutal slayings in Tobe Hooper's Texas Chainsaw Massacre, and as psychologically complex as Silence of the Lambs; a film which, funnily enough, Romero has a cameo in. It's a very intelligent, deep character study, and also a reflection of teenage isolation, loneliness and despair, feelings which for the luckier ones tend to leave our systems as we leave our teens. Is Martin the ultimate teenage nightmare?

"I was struck by Martin's isolation," Amplas said, emphasising the character's predicament. "His obvious sense of being different. Of not being able to fit in. Of having an obsession, an addiction that he himself did not fully understand the source of. Without going into my own life experiences, let's just say I readily related to these characteristics. Remember, too, I had both the screenwriter and the director to guide me. Once you start shooting, it's all about playing each moment as clearly and effectively as you can within the given circumstance."

Most importantly though, Romero sees it as his one defining picture and urges us all, especially those who see him as "that zombie guy" to seek it out and give it a try. While there is room for all Romero's work, Martin is something special indeed.

"It's my favourite," he told the Telegraph. "It never had any sort of distribution at all. And the same thing happened with Knightriders. But you know what, with home video now, I go to these conventions, and I sign more Martin DVDs than anything else. And Knightriders. It's amazing. So people have rediscovered, or discovered for the first time. It's wonderful. I just wish they would have showed up when it first played. You know, I've made six zombie films, I've tried consciously to make each one different from the next. But that's not what people want these days. They want the same thing! I don't know if that's part of this television mentality, where people tune in every week to see the same thing. I don't know."

DAWN OF THE DEAD (1978)

Undoubtedly the most iconic and popular of the Dead trilogy, Dawn of the Dead really captured the public's imagination upon its 1978 release and has gone down in history as a film classic. Those involved with the picture often ask themselves why the film has endured and why it made such a big impact on audiences, but the truth is no matter how one might dissect and ponder on the matter, there is no real explanation as to why any film endures the test of time. Maybe the whole idea of the shopping mall as a safe haven appealed to the masses? Perhaps the fantasy of having free reign of all those shops and all that stuff, as the characters in the film do, struck a chord with everyone? Maybe the fact that the zombies were surrounding the mall, still roaming the shops even after they were dead, intrigued a generation on the cusp of a massive consumerism wave? Or maybe they just thought it was a great horror film! George was clearly on to something very thought provoking, using the vast materialistic arena as a device in a sharp and concise sociological statement, right before shopping centres and indoor malls were all the rage.

After visiting the Monroeville Mall in Pittsburgh, which was owned by some of his friends, Romero latched on to the idea that a real zombie epic could be put together with excellent results in such a huge setting. When his friend had casually remarked, in a joking manner, that you could survive a nuclear apocalypse in the mall, Romero added "or a zombie apocalypse!" There was so much to use in there that the film could go a huge step beyond the small scale claustrophobia of Night of the Living Dead.

Soon after Romero had come up with the germ of his idea, almost simultaneously in fact, horror film director Dario Argento called George and asked him if he would be interested in making a follow up his 1968 zombie classic. It is true that George had never really had the desire to make a sequel and had resisted doing so for almost ten years, despite numerous offers. "I resisted going to Hollywood to make a sequel for a studio," he said. "I've always been a maverick that way and chosen to work independently."

With the prospects of the mall in mind, Romero agreed to Argento's offer, realising that he could use the urgency of the genre to put across some straight to the-point, biting social satire. Argento visited New York to meet with Romero (whose work he admired) in a bid to sort out a deal. Before he knew it, Romero was in Rome with Argento, staying in a small apartment (along with girlfriend and wife- to-be Christine) writing the script to what would become Dawn of the Dead. With Argento financing the project, the Italian was free to make a cut for European audiences once the film was released, but not once did he mess with Romero's script. He would visit Romero every two days, bring in a translator to adapt it in order to understand the progress and would then leave him to it. He did however remove some of the humour from the film in his European edit, but seeing as this was Dario Argento, there is no real surprise there. As a result of Dario cutting out much of the humour, making the picture seem wholly more bleak and violent as a whole, the censors came down hard on that version when it was ready to be released. Romero's cut however, with much of the social commentary and jokes more evident, went down much better and his edit received much less criticism from the censors as a result.

Whereas George has said that much of the underlying satirical elements in Night of the Living Dead were accidental, he has admitted that in Dawn of the Dead they were there in the script from the word go. The satire on consumerism was one of his first ideas when writing the film and all through the script there are sly jibes and pokes at the reliance of man on their material objects. "Why are they here?" is asked in one scene. "Instinct... memory" is the reply. There is also a line about this being an important place to them.

"We want all this stuff," Romero said. "And getting it, not only is it not enough... somebody else wants it too. Aside from all the other themes that run through, a lack of communication, an inability to organise; you know, things I always work with, like the media. Ignoring the fact that there is a problem and just try and ignore it."

When the story begins, the Living Dead are starting to spread big time and the whole world is in a state of panic. The movie begins with commotion at the WGON television studio in Philadelphia.

Stephen, who works there, is the pilot of the station's helicopter with a plan to steal the chopper, a plot which his girlfriend Francine is also up for. They meet Roger, a SWAT team member who has been wiping out zombies in an infested apartment block. Persuaded to come aboard them in their escape route, the three of them, along with fellow SWAT member Peter, flee Philadelphia. They eventually find safety in a shopping mall, after coming across countless more members of the Living Dead, and barricade themselves inside for most of the duration of the film. It is not until the end when a gang of violent bikers invade the mall that their plan is ruined by the ensuing mayhem. Francine and Peter finally escape in their helicopter, a stirring climax accompanied on the soundtrack by old fashioned, stirring movie ending strings.

The truth is, Romero's original script ended in a much more downbeat fashion, as he recalled in 2007: "I actually had all the people die in the Dawn of the Dead script. One of the things that's always bothered me about horror is that the only reason to do it is to upset the applecart, and it seems like everybody very deliberately restores order. They shoot the giant spider and it's all over. Halfway through that film, I realized I didn't *have* to restore order just to have a couple of people survive. And number two, I realized I should just let it ride. So, I threw in a lot more humour and had a little fun with it."

Coming ten years on from Night of the Living Dead, Dawn of the Dead is a much bigger and more multi layered film. Romero's wife Christine claimed the film was too big, an observation Romero combated with "I'll find a way." The zombies, while for the most part are a threat, become something of a joke before the end of the film,

54

especially to the cruel bikers who invade the mall. To them, slaying the zombies with mallets and machetes has become a game, while the pie fight further illustrates this point. In these sequences, as in other heartless scenes with the zombies, there is an air of pity for the creatures. After all, they are us, but in a more primitive, animal like way. There is a certain level of saddening innocence about Romero's zombies and as the bikers take them out with varying degrees of brutality, we find that we feel quite sorry for them, even though we shouldn't, considering what horrifying things they have done throughout the rest of the movie. Of course, the zombies eventually turn on the bikers and they meet a bloody demise, perhaps Romero's way of turning it back on the viewer so they do not forget they are still watching true terror at work.

The budget was once again very low considering usual film costs, coming in at just under a million dollars. Moving the effects and gore up a gear, Romero employed the services of Tom Savini, now a legendary figure in horror film special make up effects. Savini recalled getting the call about his possible job in the movie, commenting "We need to think of some new ways to kill people!" During the making of the film, Savini and the team would approach Romero with fresh and exciting zombie death ideas. As usual, George had an open mind for all suggestions and the effects specialists were pretty much free to try out whatever they wanted. The zombies on the other hand, often numbering up to 200, required a simply applied one shade of gray make up. In order to get through the extras, Savini was helped out by local make up and effects people and sometimes even the actors, including Joe Pilato who had a small role in the film and was one of the leads in the follow up, Day of the Dead. Savini, ever the creative one, made an interesting mix for the blood used in the film; his ingredients were peanut butter, food colouring and cane sugar syrup.

Before Dawn of the Dead, George and Tom had actually known each other for quite a while. In fact, Tom Savini had intended to do the effects to Night of the Living Dead back in 68, but when filming eventually started he had already been drafted to Vietnam where he was stationed as a war photographer.

To cast the movie, Romero began as usual by asking friends to fill the needed roles. Secondly, a casting call was held, this being where Gaylen Ross was discovered. Ross was to play Francine, but Romero was unaware of the fact that Ross had made up a fake CV in order to get the role, having no experience prior to the film and admitting she couldn't even act. As well as Ross, New York actor Ken Foree was also discovered. Seeing as he was now deliberately looking for an African American actor for the lead, Foree was perfect; strong, imposing and full of character. He had known the original Night of the Living Dead star Duane Jones for years, as the two actors both attended the National Black Theatre in New York. "Duane and I went back a long time," Foree said. "You know, when Night of the Living Dead first was released, I think in '68, I saw it playing on a marquee and I saw Duane's picture all over the front of the theatre, I said, 'My God!' So I ran up to the theatre where we (worked) and I said, 'Duane, you know you've got a movie going, it's all over the place... and hey, what is this about?' And he said, 'Shhh! Quiet, I'm trying to keep it quiet.' I don't know if Duane really realized the impact of the film. There was a lot of flack for those kinds of films back in those days. You know not everyone was a fan, a lot of people thought that it was in poor taste. You had to deal with a lot of people with their noses turned up towards you."

As for the other two leading cast members, David Emge and Scott Reininger had both been working in a restaurant when Emge had a chance meeting with a famous diner. Emge recalled that it was a simple audition with George, after which he was bluntly told he had the job. "I was doing cooking at this restaurant. I walked into work one day around 4:00 - 4:30, something like that," Emge recalled. "You had to walk through the front of the restaurant to get back to the kitchen. And this guy had these private little booths that were set up in the windows that were across the front of the building. As I came in the building and started to go through the restaurant, the owner says, "David, come here. I want you to meet somebody." And I walked over toward the table, and there were a few guys setting there. And the owner says, "David, I want to introduce you to GEORGE ROMERO." I said "Hi George. How are you doing? Good to meet you!" And finally, I wasn't probably as egregious as that, but we sort of talked for a while. I asked what he was doing in New York. He said he was putting together a film project, and was in New York doing some casting. So, I said, "Fine. Can I audition?" He said "Sure" ... so a few days later I auditioned for him for Dawn of the Dead. And I got the part."

With allowance to use one of the first ever indoor malls, each night in there filming seemed to become a kind of crazy party. Zombie extras came from all over town, each of them paid in the form of a dollar and a doughnut. Romero said that the energy of Tom Savini and the effects team created a real buzz on the set and much of the excitement was in seeing what Tom would come up with next. He even got himself a part in the movie, playing one of the bikers, Blades (named so because of his fondness for knives) at the climax of the film. He also performed numerous stunts, despite not having any prior experience of doing any. "I was a wild kid," he has since said.

Romero too, is quick to praise the man at every given opportunity. "Tom is a ball of energy. He's a great guy, but he was a genius. He was able to improvise. Making film is constantly compromising, and there are always things to come and bite you on the butt. But Tom was great with that"

The shooting progress was constant and atmosphere on set was light, energetic and jovial. Tom Savini has said it was "a blast" and "like a Halloween celebration!" Lasting all of the winter of 76/77, the filming was only stopped for three nights to make way for Christmas shopping. "Making this film today would cost millions of dollars," said Christine Romero. "Everyone was working for hardly any money... we hardly slept."

Ken Foree said the shoot was exciting, as there was so much going on all the time. He also recalled his various part of making the whole film. "I think the one that most men can relate to is jumping into the gun shop, putting on the double holsters, putting on the bandolier and coming out, and the music's going. I felt like a real Western cowboy star!"

Romero said that everybody had to put 110 percent into the project and that each and every contributor seemed to be totally immersed in the process. Christine Romero commented that she didn't remember a time when they weren't working, apart from of course when they were sleeping. As a result, the set was largely fuelled by coffee!

What must be pointed out with Dawn of the Dead is the strength of the performances from the actors and the multi layered context of their characters. Every Romero picture tends to have a real focus on the characters, perhaps this being the reason why his films are so much more rich and provocative than most flat out gory horror movies. Always casting unknowns, Romero gives inexperienced performers the room and opportunity to shine and also keeps the audience guessing as to who might survive the dreadful goings on. After all, if there had been one big star in Dawn of the Dead, the viewers would surely guess that he was to be the strongest character that outlived the rest and stood as the hero at the finale. But casting famous faces put aside, Dawn of the Dead has a fantastic ensemble, led by the on screen charisma of Ken Foree. One moment, perhaps one of the most famous in the film (and my personal favourite), involves Foree, Ross and Emge peering down from the top floor of the mall, proudly wearing the new fur coats which they have looted from one of the extravagant stores. The question is brought up as to why the creatures have suddenly appeared in the world. Foree utters the haunting line "When there is no more room in hell... the dead will walk the earth." It is another case of this unexplained phenomenon of the zombie break out. We don't know, they don't know, nobody knows why the creatures are here, but the important thing is the characters and how they react to such a turbulent situation.

The character that seems to be the main hero at the beginning of the movie is the professional and precise Roger, played by Scott Reininger. One great scene, just after the famous moment when the top of the zombie's head is removed by the propeller, involves David

Emge trying to shoot a creature that approaches him in a field. He misses, and then hits the beast's chest in a bumbling moment, until Roger bursts into the scene and gets the zombie right in the head. Emge's character is the everyday man, the type of person that most of us would be in this situation; shaking with fear. Unlike most horror and action films, in Dawn of the Dead, the guy next door doesn't suddenly become an expert in armed combat, holding a shot gun in each hand and getting his targets right in their heads every time. He struggles awkwardly and nervously through the action, while leaving it to the trained SWAT team hot shot to pick off the creatures with effortless cool. This is another way in which Romero's movies are a cut above the others. Of course, he goes one further and reverses our expectations by making Roger the limping doomed soul for a big part of the movie, after he is bitten by a zombie in the truck sequence, knowing full well that he will soon be transforming into one of the undead. But this turn of events was as a result of his sheer cockiness, arrogantly assuming that he had everything in control and was indestructible when he was not. Reininger is brilliant in his role.

Gaylen Ross, despite her lack of experience, does well too. The part as written, seeing as she was pregnant and fragile, was of a screaming, panicker, being sick down the toilet and refusing to join in the proceedings out of pure fear. But Ross refused to go with the script and decided not to scream and cry. Gaylen credits Romero's film with giving cinema "a pre Alien Sigourney Weaver-esque female lead role". It seems that another thing which Romero should be applauded for, in retrospect, is his ability to help create strong female characters.

Another one of Romero's specialties is getting you to really care about the people in his movies. Of course, this is also down to the performers, but it is ultimately the director and writer's choice that can influence the viewer's decision. Funnily enough though, in interviews Romero has often noted that the "theme" itself comes first to him, the basic premise of what he is going to be saying in the film, while the characterisation comes second, or even last. "I don't care about that stuff," he joked.

Although Romero loves to direct, he has often claimed that the editing part is his favourite experience when making a movie. It is a time to sit back and ponder the work you have done, and it is also the point when a film really begins to take shape. His assistant editor Pasqualle Buba said that Romero is a force of nature in the editing room and it is a joy to watch him at work in there. When observing the cuts in the film, one can see that without Romero's careful and precise editing, Dawn of the Dead would have been a much lesser film.

When viewing the film, it is clear that once again Romero is using that famous "cover your ass" filming style, ensuring that every scene is properly filmed at every realistically conceivable angle. We are invited into the action once again, perhaps more so than in the film's predecessor. It's clean, multi layered and not missing a decent shot. The difference here though in Romero's directorial style, as opposed to the one used in Night of the Living Dead, is that the film is given a deliberate "comic book" style. In truth, this had been Romero's aim from the start, to create a broader, almost dream like atmosphere; perhaps this was to ease people from the often grotesque violence that he would be throwing at them throughout the film. The "comic book" look is also enhanced by the zombies themselves; here in colour for the first time in all their grey faced glory.

Getting Dawn of the Dead released in the US proved to be tough work for Romero. Many distributors turned it down and those who did show interest in it wished to cut out the gore heavily. But Romero and Rubinstein refused to back down, sticking with their vision the whole way through. Eventually, they had the film shown at the Olympia Theatre, where it apparently blew the roof off. As a result of its terrific reaction, United Film Distribution decided to release the film.

When it finally hit the cinemas, reaction to the film was way above everybody's expectations. Eventually making 55 million dollars world wide at the box office, the film also received rave reviews from the critics and was hailed as a satirical masterpiece. Even to this day, it is named one of the best films of the 70s, a mean feat for a genre picture; it was ambitious, witty and brutally resonant. Luckily Romero managed to not get the film an X rating (it went by without a rating) so the film did wider business world wide, notably excelling in Europe and the UK. Reactions were typically varied. People were known to throw up, while others reacted with delight. (Scott Reininger took his grandma to see the film, who predictably asked to leave the theatre as soon as the Puerto Rican man's head was blown off.)

If there is one thing that comes out at you in this film, aside the gore, then it is George's message against greed and the sheer ridiculousness of mass consumerism. While criticisers of the film mock the obviousness of the satire, Romero wrecks their jibes by admitting that the message is not meant to be underlying. It is, in fact, intended to be very much in-your-face. Romero was obviously taking shots at the way the media tells us we "need" these items, which will apparently make our lives more worthwhile. These shots that had to be clearly defined in the film other wise there would have been no point making them. Romero was not afraid to ruffle a few feathers it seems. Why are *we* so easily led by the powers that be? Why do we think these "things" are so essential and how much of our personal taste is in fact down to our own choice? We are all zombies.

If people missed or cared very little about any possible slices of social satire, then fair enough, because Dawn of the Dead also stands up as an exciting piece of entertainment. There is much to chew on for the intellectuals and much to get off on for the gore freaks!

"We had made a crowd pleaser," Romero recalled. "Those were golden days."

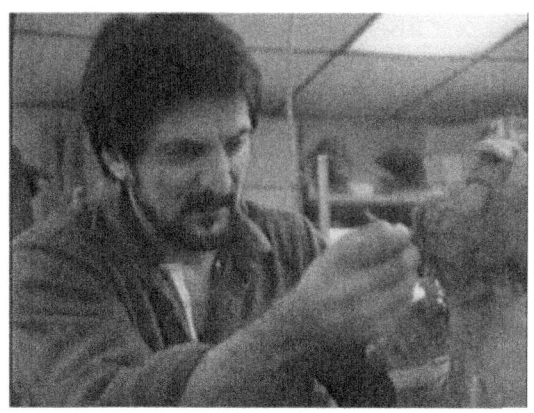

AN INTERVIEW WITH TOM SAVINI
(MAKE UP AND SPECIAL EFFECTS)

You were a combat photographer in Vietnam. Did any films about the war really capture anywhere near what it was like out there?

Platoon came pretty close and not surprising as Oliver Stone is a Vietnam vet, but also surprising to me that he didn't put in little details that no one knows about unless they've been there like how we moved Vietcong bodies out of the way with como wire, waiting till rigor set in to put one wire behind the head and another around the feet to lift and toss them into trucks. The Deer Hunter had some very real emotional editing in it when one minute they are having fun in the states, and the very next minute they are there in the Jungle. This is how it felt. You didn't believe you were there, and that jump in time was real and felt real to me when I saw it. Full Metal Jacket was the best as far as the feeling of really being there.

How did you journey from war photographer to special effects?

That's a misconception and I'm tired of it. My career in special make up effects did NOT begin in Vietnam. It started when I was 11 years old with my interest in make up effects, and characters, and old age, and monsters. Vietnam was simply for me a lesson in anatomy. You know, seeing the real thing, the real destruction to a human being mutilated and exploded and fucked up. My safety net was the mind set of how I would create the horrible shit I was seeing with special effects. That is what set me apart in the effects world, as I am the only make up effects artist who has seen the real thing first hand. My reputation for realism comes from that.

I read that you were lined up to do effects for Night of the Living Dead. How come you didn't end up doing the effects?

I had enlisted in the Army on the HOLD program which means there's something like 140 days or so within which they call you in. They called me in before I was able to do Night of the Living Dead.

How did you come to be employed for the make up effects for Romero's follow up Dawn of the Dead?

Well, when I returned to Pittsburgh, this is after Vietnam and being stationed at Fort Bragg in North Carolina, and after my discharge staying in North Carolina and working in theatre for seven years...

and after doing Martin with George. I was back in North Carolina doing a play, The Lion In Winter, and got a telegram from George saying "We've got another gig. Start thinking of ways to kill people." The rest is history.

How does Romero stand as a collaborator and director in comparison to other directors you have worked with on their films?

Most of the directors I've worked with were like George in that they were up for suggestions and improvisations with the make up effects. George would let you improvise as a make up man and as an actor and there was always more familiarity with George as we have worked together so often, and we're Pittsburghers so it was more like a family and you were hanging out with your friends.

Day of the Dead, at the time ignored in comparison to Dawn, is definitely the goriest of the Dead movies. Was there a conscious decision to "up" the gore?

Day is George's favourite of the Dead movies and mine too. I think it's my masterpiece as far as the gore and a shinning example of how George let me come up with stuff and then do it. Like, okay we want to tear off Taso's head. George: "Okay." Or we want to tear Joe Pilato in half. George: "Okay." Or we're thinking of taking off a zombie's head with a shovel... same response and we came up with a lot of stuff like that.

Do you think computer effects have ruined the magic?

66

When it's done badly, and on the other hand, in the hands of artists who know what they're doing, the best make up effects I see are the result of combining make up effects with CGI. I love it when it's done well, but as far as magic, that is destroyed as soon as you get behind the camera. I wish I could see a movie again through the eyes of the 10 year old child when that magic existed and everything you saw was real. It is replaced with the magic of creating. Good, but not the same.

How do you look back on your work in Romero's films?

It's what made us both famous, it was fun, it was creative, everyday was Halloween, and we are still doing appearances and every time there is a new release or someone buys one of the DVDs it's like we just did it, and new generations are discovering our work and keeping us in the spotlight.

Finally, could you describe Romero in five words if you can?

Bright, funny, charming, professional, and loyal.

KNIGHTRIDERS (1981)

Knightriders is possibly the one Romero film which sticks out from his filmography the most. It's also the film which is the least like Romero according to the public's perception of the director. It features many of the usual Romero horror suspects in performing roles, like Tom Savini, Joe Pilato, Anthony DiLeo and Ken Foree, but it is certainly not a horror picture. It is, in fact, a very personal and important film in Romero's canon.

Future film legend Ed Harris is the leader of a travelling group of bike jousting performers, a communal bunch of outlaws who live by a medieval code. When tensions start to appear in the gang, Tom Savini decides to break out and start his own group, with himself as the king. A clash between the two kings leads to a selection of sub plots involving corrupt cops, homosexuality and the most tragic ending imaginable, all done in typical Romero style.

Knightriders is interesting because it explores a very sixties sort of naive idealism, and also delivers the painful sucker punch of reality. The group desperately and perhaps stubbornly wish to keep their unrealistic existence alive, while also facing up to the fact that this is not medieval England, but modern day America. Could the film be a blurred reference to Romero's own ideals in the summer of love, the ones he knew were not only unrealistic, but impossible to obtain? He has said that Night of the Living Dead was a dark and angry retaliation against the times, with the hippy generation fading away in front of our eyes. "Where are The Beatles when you need them?" Romero once said. So is the frustration of the outsider, trying to make his own reality work in an increasingly limiting time.

"Knightriders was funny," Romero later said, "I had written a script, basically the same story, but I had them on horse back. I was pitching it around. We pitched it to Sam Arkoff, and he said 'tell you what, put the guys on motorcycles and maybe I'm interested.' Typical Sam Arkoff style. I fumed over that for months and finally I had the script, and came around to thinking 'you know, maybe that's not so crazy.' So we modernised it and brought it up to date. So I decided to go with it."

Knightriders is a personal piece to Romero, in as much that he was given free reign by Laurel Productions to explore any theme or idea he felt like, regardless of its commercial potential... just as long as it had motorbikes. In 1981, Romero was the King of the Zombies, having recently scored box office gold with Dawn of the Dead. Night of the Living Dead was only 13 years old by then, but it was already a legendary picture of its genre. To the wider public, Romero was just a one dimensional zombie film maker, and, not to sound patronising, perhaps many of the people who whooped and hollered in the cinema at the sight of zombies getting their heads blown off totally missed the subtext beneath the surface. Here, way under the radar, was a quirky, well acted and neatly put together ensemble piece which nobody took any notice of. At 2 and a half hours, it also spelt bad news for the distribution company, stuck in the position of promoting a film about jousting bikers, shot by the zombie master himself, George A. Romero. It figures.

With Knightriders, as in many of his films, Romero is very concerned with the fact that people just can't get on. It's a theme he explores continuously when dealing with an cast of varied faces and personalities; man's inability to see eye to eye, whatever the situation. In Dawn of the Dead for instance, the four survivors holed up in the mall are getting on fine, until the bikers appear to cause havoc and create a three sided war of shoot outs and flesh tearing. It's the outlook of the characters and how they choose to view the zombie apocalypse that separates them; the heroes simply want to get by and survive, while the bikers want to have a party and make a night of it. In Day of the Dead, the scientists and the military fail to get on for even a second, divided by their backgrounds, personalities and beliefs. Again, in Knightriders, Romero points out that even a gang of people supposedly with the same belief system, existing on the fringes of society, can't quite agree on every aspect of their life and it's inevitable that the leader, or in this case the king, will be overthrown. Romero is once again frustrated by humanity, or more correctly the general lack of it. And in true Romero fashion (spoiler alert), as if to prove his point, he kills off the hero in the final reel.

I see Knightriders as semi-autobiographical, as a subtle way of Romero putting himself in the spotlight. He is the outlaw, the maverick, the outsider on the borders of Hollywood, peering in, never fully accepted or embraced. After all, the biker is the ultimate rebel, the true outlaw. But Romero is a different kind of outlaw, an outcast in the truest sense. He's the man literally eaten up by the zombies he made such an important part of mainstream culture, a frustrated artist not only willing, but desperate to make a deeper film not just concerned with the living dead. Romero is thankful for the chances he has had in cinema to use horror as a vehicle to make a more important point, but he's also a moralist being munched away.

Romero was a film maker seeing out his vision against all odds, both critically and on a more literal physical level. "One of the things about George," Ed Harris later said, "when we did Knightriders, he was under a lot of pressure financially. Get a shot on time, we had some major weather problems, huge storms down there that put us back a bit. And George was working over time. He was really busting his butt to get the picture made. And so it wasn't a whole bunch of just lounging round with George. But when we worked director - actor, I remember feeling totally free to ask him whatever or suggest whatever. We tried to make the best film we could "

It sounds like a strange idea for a Romero picture, but technically and in performance it's effective. The idea of holding on to your integrity is a strong theme which many people can relate to, George especially. Underlying it all though, is the sadness of the fact that our dreams and wishes may not survive real life.

CREEPSHOW (1982)

After making a serious artistic statement with Knightriders, albeit one disguised as a biker exploitation B movie, Romero returned to his more widely accepted role as horror gore god for 1982's Creepshow. Intended as a homage to the gruesome EC Comics he so adored in his younger years, Creepshow brought in equal doses of terror and humour to make a truly unique one-off, the type of movie that has often been attempted since but never quite mastered. It's a tricky formula, and one that only a genius like Romero could pull off.

Romero had been introduced to writer Stephen King prior to this, mainly on the grounds that the production people saw similarities between King's vampire novel Salem's Lot and Romero's dark Martin. The pair hit it off and pretty soon the idea for Creepshow came about.

With a screenplay by King and direction from Romero, it was a match made in heaven... or should that be hell?

"The appeal was that I grew up with EC Comics," Romero told Sci Fi Now. "In the days before the Comics Code, when I was just a kid, there was this whole series that EC released – Tales From The Crypt, Vault Of Horror and all of that stuff – and I loved it all. Sure, they were horror stories but they were also morality tales. So when we did Creepshow, which Stephen King modelled after these great old comic books, the bottom line was that the bad guys always got their comeuppance, but he also peppered the script with some social commentary. It was a dream project."

Romero filmed Creepshow in Pittsburgh, his trusty old town, and converted an abandoned school into a film studio for the grotesque cinematic shenanigans to take shape. Again, he assembled a reliable team of experts, like old friend, FX master Tom Savini. For Savini himself, Creepshow is his personal favourite of all the movies he has worked on, and you can see why. The fact he also said it was the most challenging of his film experiences is rather telling too.

Creepshow is basically a collection of gruesome tales from the pen of our greatest horror writer, presented to the screen by one of modern horror cinema's true giants. The stories themselves are creepy for sure, but not totally terrifying or overly gruesome. They are very colourful, presented to us in comic book form with animated links between them to enhance the daring concept of the comic strip movie. Though daft, Creepshow is a delight from start to finish, a fearless, silly and utterly unforgiving slice of comic horror. The fact that Romero, once again, uses the horror movie as a device to explore the human condition is noteworthy. These are serious morals dressed as comedy thrillers, with Romero as the ironic punisher of sinners.

Given its cult status and the fact it has spawned two follow ups (one involving Romero, one not), Creepshow was not an easy film to get made. Which is surprising, when you consider that at the time King was perhaps the highest selling novelist in the world.

"In the case of Creepshow," Romero told Film Criticism, "we shopped at three studios and they all said no because it was an anthology. Today there are six anthologies shooting. It's matter of timing. I mean, two studios passed up E.T. There is a lot of bullshit in making deals. It has a lot to do with who you know."

The fact that Creepshow was tricky to get made doesn't come across in the resulting picture and its generally light tone. Indeed, despite the frequent gore and gruesome goings on, it's a strangely uplifting film. Here, Romero is not overly pissed off with anything in particular, and he isn't using film as a tool to attack the government, the social fabric, society's ills or indeed, as he perhaps had with Knightriders, his outsider, almost leper-like status in the movie world. Romero had a pretty sizeable budget to play with (8 million being massive for a Romero movie), and throughout seems to be having a lot of fun. And for once, he was given a cast of stars, such as Ted Danson and Leslie Nielsen. But the stars were not the focus for George. It was all about creating the best homage he could to those comics of his childhood.

"What I really wanted to do was make it completely static," Romero said of his techniques in capturing the comic book style, "like a comic book. We didn't want to do a lot of camera tricks. My tendency is not to move the camera. I'm not enraptured by fancy shots."

The film is bookended by a prologue and an epilogue, in which a young boy called Billy (played by Stephen King's son Joe), is punished by his dad for reading a horror comic. Then the boy, and the viewer of course, are lured into the grizzly world of the Creep, starting with the first tale, Father's Day, where an evil murdered dad returns from the grave to get his revenge. The second story, and possibly the funniest of the lot, stars Stephen King as Jordy Verrill (a performance which the New York Times unfairly summed up as "owing a lot to the set decorator"), a hopeless yokel who gets infected by a crashed meteorite and meets a gruesome end. The best story, for me at least, is Something To Tide You Over, in which Leslie Nielsen buries his wife and her lover up to their necks on the beach, and is then visited by their half decomposed bodies. The next story focuses on a mysterious crate which holds a mysterious Yeti-like beast, and the final tale is a truly cringe worthy one centred on a horde of cockroaches.

Creepshow cleverly centres itself on many of our most common fears, and injects them with humour and high camp. It's not the kind of film you'd have to be worried about watching on your own, but is also the kind of feature enjoyed best with friends or family, all gathered round the TV to take in the ludicrous sights and sounds. Again, like with Dawn of the Dead, Romero made a crowd pleasing romp. In his book on Romero's movies, author Tony Williams claims that the film hangs too much hope on the viewer's familiarity with EC Comics, and adds that anyone not experienced in the realm of the comic book might be baffled by the film's presentation. Suggesting it as a novel approach though seems to diminish how original, clever and inventive Creepshow really is. As someone from Northern

England, born in the mid 1980s and not remotely familiar with EC Comics until reading interviews with Romero himself (when he repeatedly refers to them as his inspiration no less), I could not have been a less ideal viewer if the film really was aimed at EC Comic buffs. Credit must go to King and Romero for crafting a success of a potentially misguided idea, and making a very alternative piece of American culture totally accessible and inclusive for all viewers.

Reviews were great too, with many critics singling it out as a decent offering. Roger Ebert gave it 3 out of 4, but then he had always been a Romero fan anyhow. "Creepshow plays like an anthology of human phobias," Ebert pointed out. "What could be more horrifying that sticking your hand into a long-forgotten packing crate and suddenly feeling teeth sink into you? Unless it would be finding yourself buried up to the neck on the beach, with the tide coming in? Or trapped in an old grave, with the tombstone toppling down on top of you? Or having green stuff grow all over you? Or how about being smothered by cockroaches? The horrors in Creepshow are universal enough, and so is the approach. Romero and King have approached this movie with humour and affection, as well as with an appreciation of the macabre. They create visual links to comic books by beginning each segment with several panels of a comic artist's version of the story, and then dissolving from the final drawn panel to a reality that exactly mirrors it. The acting also finds the right note."

In comparison to earlier horror anthologies, say the British ones made by Amicus (The Vault of Horror, Tales from the Crypt), Creepshow is less straight faced and it's all the better for it. Romero proved he had a knack for short story telling and getting to the point quick on the screen. He would be partly (*very* partly in fact) responsible for one of the best horror series of the 1980s, the brilliant Tales from the Darkside, writing a number of episodes but mostly just having his name above the title like a deadly blessing. (He would also be a part of its cinematic adaptation, but more of that later.) But Creepshow is something special, the kind of film that only comes along every so often, where each ingredient is perfectly mixed to make sublime results. Mad, hilarious, shiver inducing stuff.

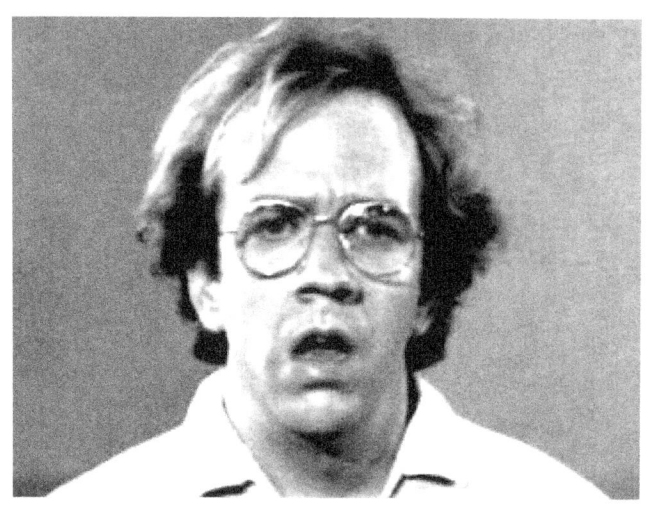

AN INTERVIEW WITH ROBERT HARPER
(CHARLIE GERESON IN CREEPSHOW)

How did you come to be in Creepshow?

My agent arranged a meeting with the casting people from Laurel Entertainment and the director, George A. Romero. The company was in from Pittsburgh and there was a very "low-key" quality to the project - it was not a "Hollywood" production - and when I met Mr. Romero at this time, he explained that he and Stephen King had loved EC comics as kids, and they wanted to recreate the feelings they recalled having. He explained that he wanted to do the film as a comic book. He referred to the violence in the script as something that would be "stylized" in shades of red - just like the comic books which inspired it. It would not be "gruesome" in the theater, but rather "creepy."

I was a bit younger than either Romero or King, but our real difference growing up was that I was a product of a home that frowned upon comic books; comic books weren't allowed in the house! There was a book out in the 1950's that had an effect on my parents and many others called the "Seduction of the Innocent." It painted comics as capable of creating juvenile delinquents. There is a book out in the past few years about this – called, I think, The 10 cent Plague.

What was it like to be directed by a master like George A. Romero?

I found George Romero to be a kind, accessible man, who spoke softly, didn't seem to have a big ego or a sense of self importance and relied on a low key approach to the material. He was open to suggestions and willing to let the actor take the time to feel comfortable. In musical terms, he reminded me of a lead jazz player who expects you to know the notes, and who encourages an individual riff within the structure established. He also used a one-on-one way of talking with the actors.

One of the next films you did was Once Upon A Time In America, directed by Sergio Leone. That must have been so different from working with George. How did the two directors differ from one another?

Sergio Leone is more like a maestro with an orchestra. We filmed in Italy with an Italian speaking crew and spoke an Italian version of English with Sergio. I was the new kid on the block; I had worked a couple of years earlier with Treat Williams on a Broadway revival of Once in a Lifetime, but I was also to be the "heavy" in a scene with experienced pros like Robert De Niro and James Woods. It would be accurate to say that I was nervous and not entirely confident on my first day. DeNiro was already an enormous star, yet open and helpful; he made me feel comfortable. Sergio was very clear on what he wanted, always aware of the "big" picture. He has an acute eye and can watch numerous takes, noticing the smallest variations. He spoke to us as a group, as a conductor might guide the wind section, say. There was a formality and "size" that was different than the lower key, softer approach of the work in Pittsburgh.

What did you think of the finished film once you saw it?

I had the treat of seeing the premiere at a big theater in mid-Manhattan which seated maybe 1200 - 1500 people. The audience had lots of gasps and laughs and during the final sequence – with E.G. Marshall and the roaches – the place went absolutely bananas – screaming throughout. I thought the film was great fun and expertly made. My recollection is that it brought in about 8 million dollars the opening weekend (about 20 million in today's dollars) so everyone was happy and expected more. I think though that all the fans came out that first weekend so it never racked up the numbers that get headlines. Through the years however, it has gathered a lot of fans through word of mouth. I thought the HBO series, Tales from the Crypt merely ripped off Creepshow.

DAY OF THE DEAD (1985)

Romero described Day of the Dead upon its release as "a tragedy about how a lack of human communication causes chaos and collapse even in this small little pie slice of society." This mental meltdown of communication just happened to be going on in the most claustrophobic, dark and depressing of settings. Whereas Dawn of the Dead provided viewers with the varied and colourful scope of the shopping mall, Day of the Dead had its characters, depressed and drained, bickering in a smelly, darkly lit underground mine. Any humour that had been present in Dawn of the Dead (the pie fight for instance) was totally absent in Romero's next feature. The only laughs in the 1985 follow up are to be had are in watching Dr Logan (Richard Liberty) training the domesticated zombie Bub (played by Howard Sherman) how to enjoy human pleasures. The film is foul mouthed, at times sickeningly gory and absolutely brilliant. For me, a true *tour de force* of intelligent horror.

Romero has said that while Night of the Living Dead appeals to the zombie purists, and Dawn of the Dead has become the "party" zombie movie, Day of the Dead is adored by "the trolls". By that of course he means the real gore nuts, the folk who crawl out from under their rocks to delight in some unforgiving zombie violence. Not to say Day of the Dead is not brilliant, it is just way more down beat, grim and in-your-face than its predecessors. It's my personal favourite of all six Dead films.

The plot focuses on a group of survivors living underground in a mine shaft, well away from the masses of zombies that roam free outside in the real world. On one side of the camp are the more sympathetic characters, the supposedly humane and scientific department who have a view to tame the creatures rather than destroy them. Lori Cardille plays Sarah, our guide through the chaos of the picture, who is in the middle of some advanced scientific research which can hopefully one day reverse the zombie process. At the other end we have the military point of view, which is a more primal stance against the zombie invasion; in basic terms, the army want the beasts dead, to do "nothing but drop over". The military merely put up with the eccentric Dr Logan's experiments because they believe, for some time at least, that they have to. They are led by Joe Pilato's wonderful creation, Captain Rhodes, who is never short of an unpleasant expletive or put down. After tensions flare and build to an uncontrollable level, the conflict between the two camps eventually takes over and the battle of morals ultimately ruins their alleged safe haven. The film climaxes in one of the bloodiest and most powerful ways a horror film could ever end.

Romero went way down with Day of the Dead to a very small scale, especially when comparing it to the vast canvas of Dawn of the Dead. But once again it was circumstance and not mere artistic vision that orchestrated the changes. Initially, Romero had been given a 7 million dollar budget and the original screenplay shows a much bigger and more extravagant movie than the one that eventually hit the big screen. When the budget was halved, Romero found himself forced to downscale the production. What he couldn't have, he made up for in other smarter ways. Action scenes in the script, including one at the harbour involving a huge gun fight with the zombies, had to be cut and replaced with more realistic sequences that fit the budget. For instance there was supposed to be an above ground camp site for the characters, but this was also scrapped due to a shortage of funds. As a result of such cuts, many of the people involved in the film remain disappointed with the results to a certain degree, bearing in mind what the end film could have been, had the original screenplay been used. But in retrospect the limitations probably made this a better film. As George has said, more money would have meant more supervision from the big wigs funding it. In exchange for less cash he was ultimately given more freedom, the opportunity to push the gore and not worry about an X rating (they were less liable to put up more money for an X rated picture back then). "I simplified it," Romero said. "I brought it down to what its essentials were." Producer Cletus Anderson said Romero put real anger into the script, anger was perhaps a result of having his large ambitions swept out from underneath him.

Romero had planned this to be "The Gone with the Wind of zombie movies" (Special effects man Tom Savini called the original script "Ben Hur with zombies!") but the results are far from epic, which is all for the better in my opinion. Whereas Dawn of the Dead had gone BIG, its follow up returned to the "trapped" atmosphere of Night of the Living Dead, by far scarier and more impressive when looking back some 25 years on. But the script went under big changes and most of the original characters were written out and replaced before the finished product saw the light of day. Romero though, once again, focused his attention, at least symbolically, on the things of the era that bugged him. He was giving up on the government, could see a real downward spiral in morals, and once again he reflected a breakdown of civil communication.

Shooting mostly took place in an underground mine shaft in Pennsylvania, the humidity of the location making the process very difficult for cast and crew. The facility was used to store important documents, but also had caves and a few lakes within its depths. Crew found the place creepy and also said it stunk of mould. Rather fittingly too, the logo for the mine used a picture of the Greek mythological figure Medusa, with wild snakes hissing out of her hair.

Filming began in October and ended in December of 1984 at Beaver Falls, with an additional two months shooting at Fort Myers. The special effects team, led once again by the charismatic and gifted Tom Savini, had prepared the numerous gore effects between the months of July and October in Savini's home basement. Effects man Greg Nicotero said that they worked on assembling props and sets that fit with the first draft for over two months, until the screenplay was altered and their attention was put into the new plot.

84

Of the first three Romero zombie movies, Day of the Dead received the most negative critical response and was seen as something of a let down in general. Money wise also, it came nowhere near to the success of Dawn of the Dead. Fans of Romero's work and the horror genre in general however loved the film and it soon entered the canon of classic zombie flicks. Critics though were cruel and claimed the film was sexist and according to The New York Times it was full of "windy argument". Criticism pointing out that the film was demeaning to women was denied by its lead actress Lori Cardille, who openly claimed her character was strong and intelligent. It is true that in most horror movies, women are either scared bimbos fleeing the creature as their clothes drop off or depicted as gun wielding tom boys. In comparison to the usual trends, Lori's performance is strong and assured, and she is the one sole character we understand the most in this dark journey.

The movie shocked many people, most notably and memorably The United States Conference of Catholic Bishops Office for Film and Broadcasting. Their appalled statement included the following damnation: "Romero's third low budget zombie chiller provides a loathsome and unimaginative mix of violence, blood, gore and some sexual references to demeaning women." Not big fans then presumably?

Robert Ebert, who had previously been very complimentary about George's movies, had little good to say about the new instalment. "The zombies in Day of the Dead are marvels of special effects", he wrote. "Truth to tell, they look a lot better than the zombies in Night of the Living Dead, which was director George Romero's original zombie film. His technology is improving. But the zombies have another problem in Day of the Dead: They're upstaged by the characters who are supposed to be real human beings. You might assume that it would be impossible to steal a scene from a zombie, especially one with blood dripping from his orifices, but you haven't seen the overacting in this movie. The characters shout their lines from beginning to end, their temples pound with anger, and they use distracting Jamaican and Irish accents, until we are so busy listening to their endless dialogue that we lose interest in the movie they occupy. Maybe there's a reason for that. Maybe Romero, whose original movie was a genuine inspiration, hasn't figured out anything new to do with his zombies. In his second zombie film, the brilliant Dawn of the Dead, he had them shuffling and moaning their way through a modern shopping mall. The effect was both frightening and satirical. This time, though, Romero has centred the action in a visually dreary location - an underground storage cavern, one of those abandoned salt mines where they store financial records and the master prints of old movies. In the earlier films, we really identified with the small cadre of surviving humans. They were seen as positive characters, and we cared about them. This time, the humans are mostly unpleasant, violent, insane or so noble that we can predict with utter certainty that they will survive. He (Romero) should quit while he's ahead."

Ebert's points are understandable, and he like many others was clearly disappointed by the film in comparison to the more upbeat and varied comic book delight of Dawn of the Dead. But the characters, as he points out, are not supposed to be likable. No one is going for points in this movie; theirs is a pitifully desperate situation and the constraints of the setting are causing them to behave like little more than animals. I thought Ebert might have understood such a realistic portrayal of human desperation.

While it had a somewhat muted response, especially in comparison to its predecessor, Day of the Dead still managed to make over ten times its budget at the box office upon release. There was still very much a healthy interest in Romero's brand of horror it seemed, even if some of the reviews were far from complimentary.

Recently Romero noted that Day of the Dead had become his personal favourite of the zombie saga. He also commented on the possible reasons why it wasn't as successful as Dawn of the Dead: "I think people wanted the same kind of romp that Dawn was. I think they just wanted it to really be... lighter, maybe? And, sillier, and have a cleaner storyline. Except for the military guy, everybody's both good and bad. It's pretty hard to calculate who you're supposed to be with (laughs). You know, it didn't have any of those traditional Hollywood movie things, and it certainly was, it was in an age when movies were beginning to really get vapid. We were going back to a sort of Western formula, almost, in different guises."

One thing that is unique about the film is its approach to the very idea of the Living Dead virus spreading all over the world. Whereas Night of the Living Dead and Dawn of the Dead showed the characters figuring out a way to survive and wipe out the creatures, Day of the Dead presents the desperately outnumbered souls trying to adapt their lives around the zombies. Cleverly, Romero provides two out looks, giving the audience the choice of whose side to be on here. The military, led by Rhodes, may be insensitive and aggressive, but I do not believe for a second they are primarily the villains of the piece. In the end, when they have finally lost all patience with the slow evolution of Logan's strange experiments (and of course when they discover he has been using one of their dead colleagues for experiments), they turn on the scientific half, killing a couple of them and leaving the others to the mercy of the zombies. To Rhodes, *he* is the good guy and them "the fucking lunatics." If referring to Logan, he does have a point. The audience though, I am sure, are supposed to support and route for Sarah and her friends, other wise why would the film hold such a happy, uplifting end for them? This is perhaps where Ebert had a point, the fact that the scientific characters were so obviously "good" that they had to survive.

Any flaws within the plot aside, the film features some of the strongest and most unforgettable scenes in horror history. The first zombie in the film, silhouetted in a close up in the abandoned town was a puppet assembled by the special effects team (it now belongs to Metallica guitarist Kirk Hammet). It is for me the most chilling start to any of the Dead films.

One scene that disturbed many viewers was the vile demise of Captain Rhodes, when he is ripped in half by the zombies at the finale of the movie. To create the sequence, a fake floor was assembled, which actor Joe Pilato sat inside up to his waist. The guts used in the scene had gone rancid as the refrigerator keeping them had somehow been switched off, but rather than getting in some new guts, they were washed down and the stench was sprayed with Old Spice. The smells from the putrid entrails had to be fanned away from Pilato during the shooting of the scene to stop him from being sick. It is a scene Pilato himself will never forget.

"We each had a day to die," he said. "Each of the Day of the Dead principal characters, that would be (Antone) DiLeo, Gary Klar and a couple of other soldiers. The effects that Savini and company created demanded quite a bit of time. The morning I walked in which was my day to die, which was also the last day of shooting because it was the most elaborate special effect, I walked in and the continuity person said, 'morning Joe, it's a good day to die' and I said 'thank you, I need to speak to George' and she said 'well he's quite busy right now'. And I said 'this is kind of important.' And, he came over and said 'what's up Joe?' and I said, 'Well, George, I don't think that Captain Rhodes would go out without saying something'. And, he said 'well let's consider the fact that your legs are being torn apart from your torso and your thorax is being ripped open, I'm not quite sure you would be able to talk'. And, I said 'well, if the fans are worried about that then we're in the wrong movie'. And then he said, 'well what do you think Rhodes would say as they're dragging your legs away?' And, I felt a little bit shy because there were other people in the room, so I said 'let me whisper it in your ear'. And this six foot four guy, and I'm only five eight, leans down and I whisper in his ear, 'choke on 'em.' And he kind of stood back and thought about it for a second and he said, 'I like it. You're right.' And it's become one of the most memorable lines. I'm also very proud of 'puss fuck,' that was a total ad-lib. 'Choke on 'em' was something thought out, but 'puss fuck'... I was crawling down the hallway as Bub is chasing me down and I really slammed my head against the concrete very hard and it hurt and I just remember yelling at Bub, 'you fuck, you puss fuck.' And when the shot was over the sound man said to George, 'did he say puss fuck?' And George said 'yeah, I like it.' So we kept it."

On that note, I believe Rhodes is one of the truly great characters of horror, as unforgiving and brutal as any disfigured killing machine monster might have been. Joe Pilato brings a real energy to the role, spitting out the foul mouthed dialogue like he really means it. We sense true desperation in his Rhodes, and whenever he is on screen we feel on edge, not knowing what the enraged Captain might do next. Pilato is brilliant in his role, and one cannot understand why he didn't go on to be a big star after this. When speaking of his audition, Pilato claimed he was thrilled to get the part and commented that he loved playing "a mean old son of a bitch!"

Lori Cardille is also fantastic in her role as one of the strongest female leads in horror history. As Sarah, she is attempting to keep her cool amidst the mayhem, the arguments and the violence. We, the viewer, are directly on her wave length, making the upset in the film all the more distressing.

Perhaps the most remembered and loved character in the film is the zombie Bub, played by Sherman Howard. As Bub is being trained to behave less primitively by the eccentric Dr Logan, his manner was set to be somewhat different to the other zombies. The only real direction Romero gave the actor for the role was to put in a bit of "infancy and innocence." Howard, under this small amount of simple guidance, constructed a more rounded character as opposed to a mere beast with a dash of likeability, and immersed himself deeply into his role. He even went as far to assume that Bub was perhaps involved in the military before he was a zombie. At one point, when Captain Rhodes enters the room, Bub salutes him, perhaps revisiting a distant memory that had lodged itself in the back of his mind. Of course, Rhodes does not salute back, a decision which eventually costs him his life. But Bub has an increasingly noticeable air of humanity about him, which Howard has really captured brilliantly.

When watching Day of the Dead, any small amount of sympathy we previously had for the creatures in previous instalments is totally over shadowed. If anything, with most of the characters in Day of the Dead being close to detestable, we find ourselves routing with the zombies, clearly a telling example of how easily our moral values can be altered to suit our own emotional comfort.

The creature has reached an interesting point in the midst of Day of the Dead, in as much that it could perhaps, in given time, return to its former self. In Dawn of the Dead, it is noted that the creatures are not cannibals because they are no longer human and that they are driven by pure instinct. So while Logan's practice was far from conventional, he was perhaps on to something, a long road that may have resulted in the reversal of the "zombie" state. It is unfortunately something that Logan never got to find out. But Bub has now reached an iconic status in zombie fandom. Even Romero himself commented that Bub had become "the quintessential, mainstream zombie."

Another stand out performance for me comes from Gary Klar who plays Steel, the tough guy soldier built like a brick shit house. He is also given some of the best dialogue, in what is definitely Romero's finest script. The words really reflect the panic and helplessness of the people in this hell. Theirs is an ugly existence, constantly on the brink of meltdown and this is reflected in the equally ugly dialogue; there is tension, jealousy, sexual frustration, machismo and greed. Few horror movies capture uncontrollable emotion in a truthful way as Day of the Dead does. While there are true elements here, regarding the lack of a proper understanding and communication,

Romero really brings to life the feelings one might have if the zombies really did take over the world.

AN INTERVIEW WITH LORI CARDILLE
(SARAH IN DAY OF THE DEAD)

How did George Romero get to cast you in the film?

As most fans know, my dear father, Bill Cardille (Chilly Billy) was in the original Night of the Living Dead. I was in the 8th grade when it opened. I remember going to the opening with my family. That is the first time I met George. As a kid, I HATED scary movies. I could never understand why people liked to be frightened. I was a very nervous child. Needless to say, I was in the lobby while the movie was playing. It was many years until I saw Night of the Living Dead. Fast forward to 1983. I had graduated from the same University that George went to a few years before me. Carnegie Mellon University is a wonderful school for theatre. Anyway, I was living in NYC and had already been on Broadway, two major soap operas, regional theatre and television films and pilots. I was doing a new play by Craig Lucas called, Reckless. I originated the role of Rachael Fitzsimmons, a strong female lead who comes on stage and drives the play. George was in the audience along with Richard Rubinstein. That's how we met again after about 17 years. He liked my performance and wrote the part of Sarah with me in mind.

With your dad being a horror icon, was it weird being cast in a Romero film?

Well, as I said, horror was NOT my favourite cup of tea. I still wasn't a fan at that time. I was into being an artiste dahling! Ha-ha. The whole thing was ironic really.

Day of the Dead was the goriest of the first three movies. Did you think you were making a unique film?

Let's put it this way, it was unique to me because I had never done a horror film before. I really had nothing to compare it to.

What was atmosphere like on the set?

Fun, relaxed and ridiculous in a good way. We were all serious about each of our crafts however.

What is it like working with George? Is there a way to describe his impact on a set?

George has a lot of respect for actors and he worked with us. He gave us a lot of creative freedom. George was and always has been a gentleman.

Day of the Dead was always my favourite of the films. I think it has a great script and a great ensemble cast. What was it like working with such a good cast and script?

I loved working with the other actors. Everyone came from the theatre and just that alone brings the ensemble up a few notches. The script we shot was not George's first script. The script we shot was much more character driven. George's first script had more explosions and action.

Do you have a favourite scene in the film?

Of my scenes, I like when Sarah cuts off Miguel's arm and her emotional aftermath. When she becomes more vulnerable, I think she becomes a much stronger character. I also love the scene where all of the zombies are eating the bodies in the cave. It's so dark and primitive. It's a beautiful piece of horror.

Seeing as the end is quite open to interpretation, do you think the three survivors died and that the ending is some kind of dream, or are you happy like me in believing they all got away for a happy ending?

I always hoped they got away. I'd like to see a sequel shot by George to see what happened to the three characters as they got older. At the New York premiere, the audience actually booed the ending.

Do you have any funny stories from the making of the film?

So many funny things happened but the most amusing memory that stands out for me is the juxtaposition of real life with this zombie movie. Several of us had small children on set while zombies roamed the halls in full makeup. Here's a typical picture: our children eating in the lunchroom next to zombies ... get the picture?

You do some of the fan conventions with other cast members. Do you enjoy meeting fans and seeing the old cast?

I do enjoy meeting the fans for sure! I find the Day fans rather thoughtful, respectful and intelligent. It's nice to say a big thank you to the fans. I also love hanging with my cast mates! Some of us are still very close friends.

AN INTERVIEW WITH JOE PILATO
(CAPTAIN RHODES IN DAY OF THE DEAD)

25 years on do you think Day of the Dead is finally getting the credit it deserved?

Yes, I do. We were side blasted by Dawn of the Dead. Everybody wanted the shopping mall and we gave them the cave under some budgetary restrictions. George keeps saying it's one of his favourite films. It had a very claustrophobic situation and you had characters coming from a complete point of view. So, it stands and it will always stand because not only is it horrific, not only does it make you 'stay scared,' it's also intellectually complete and George took what he had – his budget was cut in half – and he chose to go into the world of isolation. What he couldn't do visually he did "literally." He had points of view in collision: Logan, the mad scientist; Sarah, the buffer; Rhodes, the military man whose job was just to exterminate. So, it was a sense of confinement and ideas. People were not stupid.

George took a sense of confinement, which was opposed to his original script. He took a sense of confinement and claustrophobia where it met mindlessness. I personally think we were originally dismissed by the press for not repeating the shopping mall scenario but instead we continued with the evolution of the story.

Why do you think it was not as well received when it was released?

For Dawn, the concept of the shopping mall at that point in time was so ingenious. But nobody concentrated on the shopping mall. They concentrated on the characters. The concept of the shopping mall was brand new at the time and a sociological statement. When you look at Land of the Dead, it's about time shares. And, I don't think George starts with these concepts. You look at Dawn and it's the shopping mall and if you look at Land it's either about assisted living or timeshares. I don't think any great writer or director starts with a concept. I think George had a story to tell and the zombies had to evolve. If you create a species like George did, and you want to continue the story, there's an evolution. Look at Dawn of the Dead then look at Land of the Dead and you traverse between the shopping mall and you see the journey to timeshare. With Day, I think at the time the claustrophobic concept was lost on audience's expectations for another Dawn.

How does it feel to be part of horror history?

It really feels great. Not because of any sort of infatuation of always being accessible on DVD and other formats. The thing is the genre fans. I have never met a genre fan I didn't like. Genre fans ask great questions. In so many ways, a family has developed, and without that family, I'm just a piece of celluloid. I have the great fortune, as well as many of my colleagues do, of having an astute and knowledgeable film family. Because of the film, I'll be around for a longtime. But, it's the genre fans that have been a big part of the experience. They are the people that make this thing tick, and I love them to death. With them, we are an ongoing experience and I sincerely believe that.

Do you ever see any of the rest of Day of the Dead's cast?

Yes, absolutely. I stay in contact with all of them. I'm really close with everyone. We meet up at conventions. It's always a great celebration. Geographically, we live in very different locations. Gary, Lori, Tim and Jarlath are on the East coast, I'm on the West coast so we meet at conventions and when we do it's a wonderful thing. I speak with them by phone at least once or twice a month. It's funny because not until – let's see the movie was made in 1984... until Fangoria did a reunion years later, I hadn't seen Gary or Lori since we made the movie but have stayed in touch with them ever since. They have been a great resource in my life and I believe I've been a great resource in their lives and that doesn't happen very often in film. We spent a lot of time underground and got close. And we're still close.

So it's silly to ask if you ever get tired of being tied to Romero's films?

Absolutely not. I had the opportunity to work with one of the greatest directors whose work is in the archives of the New York Museum of Modern Art.

Finally, what is your view on Rhodes as a character and do you really think he was such a bad guy?

Rhodes was not a bad guy. You go to the airport today you either get put in a chamber or strip searched or hand searched. This is the beauty of George. Rhodes is the military point of view. Sarah and Logan were the medical point of view. It's a tough choice, we live in a tough time. I think Rhodes was like, 'shoot 'em in the head,' and that's always going to be the military point of view. Unfortunately, Major Cooper died, Rhodes would have been second in command but when Cooper died, Rhodes had to take over and it was 'Alright. Kill 'em. Don't domesticate them.' In the small circle of isolation, we had the scientific point of view, voodoo point of view – which came from Terry's character, and of course the military point of view. And, that was the job I was given. I'm not so sure I believe it today AND I'm not so sure I don't believe it today. Strip search me at the airport - I'd rather do that than go through the box because of the radiation - but protect me. George was always a visionary.

CREEPSHOW 2 (1987)

The first Creepshow movie had been a gloriously fun collaboration between two of America's greatest horror masters, so given Holywood's habit of wanting to make more profits, it was inevitable that a follow up was on the cards. However, Creepshow 2 is not quite the follow up that fans of the first might have had in mind. For one, Romero wasn't directing - Michael Grnick was taking up that role - and Stephen King, although allowing his stories to be filmed, did not write the screenplay. This was left to Romero, and as great a writer for the screen he is, he does have his own unique filming style (the cover your ass technique as he might have said), and is the only man who can really bring his ideas to life. That said, Creepshow 2 is a good old fashioned romp, featuring it does a collection of chilling tales, a host of familiar faces and top notch special effects, once again executed by the genius himself, Tom Savini.

Whereas the first movie had five tales, the sequel only has three, the best of which just has to be the last, The Hitchhiker (featuring a cameo by Stephen King as a truck driver). One story which was left off the film was a brilliant Romero story, The Cat From Hell, which thankfully finally made it to the screen in 1990's Tales from the Darkside movie.

As a result of the shorter running time, only half the budget of the first film, the lack of famous faces and without Romero in the directing role, Creepshow 2 does feel like the half hearted bastard child, and as entertaining as it is, it does not measure up at all to its predecessor. Sure, the effects are good, the humour is to the fore front and the acting is suitably broad, but there is little here that makes it worthy of the Creepshow name.

Still, it's a hell of a lot better than Creepshow 3, a film which surfaced in 2007 but did not feature any input from King or Romero. It was rightly panned and is not widely accepted as a proper addition to the franchise. (That credit goes to Tales from the Darkside, which Tom Savini claims is the real third entry of the trilogy.) As interesting and entertaining as Creepshow 2 is, it's still not a major part of his essential filmography, though worth watching for any horror or Romero buff.

MONKEY SHINES (1988)

Romero goes mainstream in 1988's Monkey Shines, a peculiar and well put together adaptation of Michael Stewart's novel. Released by Orion pictures, this was the first time George had worked with a studio, who gave him a healthy seven million dollar budget for the project. Telling the tragic tale of Allan (Jason Beghe), an athlete who becomes disabled after a truck accident, the film moves into truly surreal territory when our depressed hero teams up with Geoffrey (John Pankow), a scientist chum who has been toying with human brains and monkeys. To assist his old pal, Geoffrey gives him a monkey, Ella, who begins to help him in his daily life. Of course, the relationship is only positive for so long and the monkey soon becomes untrustworthy. Jealousy and telepathy get in the way of their bond, resulting in devastating circumstances.

First off, the plot is hopelessly daft and typical of a B movie flick of the 80s, but this isn't a B movie in its presentation. The credit of the film's minor success must go to Romero and his often overlooked versatility, a man who has proved time and time again that he can deliver the goods in a wide range of subject matters. He makes this potentially silly film work with decent pacing, which at first seems slow, but actually gives us time to develop feelings for the characters. Second off, the performances are very good and Romero ensures we are kept up close to the emotional developments between man and chimp, not least the complexities in Ella and Allan's relationship. Stanley Tucci gives an early stand out performance as Dr Wiseman, but anyone in their right mind has to admit that Boo the chimp steals the show as Ella.

If Romero hadn't already influenced horror cinema enough with his zombie classics, Monkey Shines could also be seen as a precursor to the terrifying monkeys at the start of Danny Boyle's 28 Days Later, where the rabid apes spread the virus. (Outbreak, the 1995 Ebola disaster flick springs to mind too.) In fact, some of the darkest moments in Monkey Shines are in the lab when the monkeys are causing mayhem and shrieking at their shrillest tones; although most of the thrills come when they're causing serious trouble, like dropping hair dryers in baths and urinating on laps. Anyone who watches this film may never look at monkeys the same way again.

As entertaining as it is though, it was another far from perfect filmic experience for the big man himself. Ferociously independent to the end, Romero had more than a little trouble with the major studio. They wanted a fun hit with a happy ending, and as you may well know, Romero has never been one for the cheesy Hollywood crowd pleasing finale. This is the man who killed his lead in Night of the Living Dead, who originally wanted the last survivor in Dawn of the Dead to blow her own head off. Making Romero shoot a happy ending is like forcing Martin Scorsese to leave out the F word. But he was not in complete control and obliged to their wishes. On top of that, masses of filmed footage were dropped to the cutting room floor, so once again Romero was left dissatisfied with the whole experience. While budgetary limitations had forced him to rethink his ultimate zombie epic vision for Day of the Dead, at least he had been free, but here the studio wanted a safer, easier to digest slice of mainstream horror. They got it, but the compromises didn't make it a hit. However, over time it's developed its own quirky cult following.

"I'm quoting George here," Tom Savini later said of the film. "I saved his ass on that movie. The real monkeys would sit there and do your taxes, make your dinner and figure out world peace. But as soon as George called 'Action' they just sat there and did nothing. So it's the mechanical monkeys and the monkey parts that we did, that did all the work. But the last 20 minutes of that movie are the most suspenseful you've ever seen. Anyone can jump up and shout Boo, but the scares in Monkey Shines were drawn out. they were suspense scares."

By the late 80s, George was seen as one of the most influential people in horror, but his film experiments were becoming more and more frustrating and unrewarding. He had left the independent film company Laurel after Day of the Dead, and his Orion deal looked more hopeful, at least at the start. Here was a film which examined man's egocentric urge for power, in this case over nature and science; a nice meaty subject for Romero the social commentator. The doctor in Monkey Shines, not as likeable as Day of the Dead's Logan (played by the wonderful Richard Liberty), makes the same mistake the scientists and investors made in Jurassic Park a few years later; toying with nature and seeing it turn around and quite literally bite them in the arse. Unusually for George though, there seemed very little else hanging on the film but shallow scares and thrills. (Although you could argue that he handles one of his usual themes, people struggling to get through a situation that is out of their control.) In an era where gory slasher films were beginning to take over the horror genre, social satire and subtle subtext were a thing of the past. In fact, mainstream cinema as a whole had started to become more shallow than ever, with blockbusters and scare fests offering little food for thought. Romero, a child of the sixties and a son of rebellion, seemed out of place in this excessive decade of greed and emptiness. Monkey Shines is very much of its era, but as it features the famously tasteful direction and intelligent scripting of Romero, it also fails to blend in with that rather crass age.

Romero has a lot of lost gems in his filmography, some of which are much more effective than others. A film like There's Always Vanilla for instance kind of deserves its obscure status (even George won't say much good about it), while other buried classics like The Crazies and Knightriders are now seen as minor classics in their own right. Monkey Shines however doesn't seem to be getting its much deserved reappraisal. Despite underperforming at the box office, it was acclaimed. For instance, Jonathan Rosenbaum of the Chicago Reader wrote "in between these soggy slices of bread the Monkey Shines sandwich is packed with meat, an imposing family melodrama full of faces, tension, strong feelings, and personalities, and very little wasted motion, culminating in what is probably the most protracted and successful suspense set piece in any movie this year. What the movie occasionally lacks in slickness it more than makes up in content and intensity — the maverick Romero's two calling cards ever since his Night of the Living Dead opened 20 years ago."

Some hold it with very high regard. In 2000, Empire Magazine gave it a 5 star review, and raved about its many glories. "George Romero has never quite managed to regain the heights he attained with Night Of The Living Dead, his low budget, black and white horror flick that went on to become one of the most imitated and influential films of its kind in the last 20 years. Romero, it was muttered, was yesterday's man. Monkey Shines will surely change any such premature judgement. It's a superb adaptation of Michael Stewart's interesting but rather pedestrian book of the same name. What makes all this work so well is that Romero genuinely explores the plight of the victim and his family, and grounds his characters so skilfully that by the time the extended climax comes — and it seems to go on for ever — it is all utterly convincing. There's some splendid dark humour along the way, a host of fine, solid performances, and, best of all, a near-perfect love scene nailed down second by second, in which, heartbreakingly, the hero can only move his head. By skipping on any predictable creature effects and concentrating instead on the people involved and what moves them, George Romero, with Monkey Shines, has built a reputation-restoring film of genuine emotion and character.

TALES FROM THE DARKSIDE:
THE MOVIE (1990)

Though the film anthology itself was released in 1990, Romero had been involved with Tales from the Darkside since 1983, when its name sake series was first aired. After Creepshow proved to be a modest hit back in 82, making some decent profits, a television series was briefly a possibility. Due to ownership issues with other film companies, a series was not possible. Instead, Laurel (the film company George worked with in that era) developed a similar idea, this one presented to us by George A. Romero. And so, Tales from the Darkside was born.

There were some fabulous episodes during that five year run, with many a notable guest star popping up here and there. The stories were creepy but camp, and in true Creepshow style, they were more daft than scary. However, they are all ludicrously enjoyable, especially the ones which Romero penned the screenplay for; most notably The Devil's Advocate and the pilot, Trick Or Treat.

Romero himself however doesn't associate himself too closely with the classic series. Speaking to Dread Central when the series was released on DVD, Romero exclaimed "Ain't that weird? People keep going on about it and I say I don't know anything about it, man. I wrote the pilot and three or four episodes and that was it. I don't know anything about it. I didn't know there was any love for the series. I thought it was fun and it came and went. I never thought it had a strong fan base, but apparently it does. It lasted two seasons, but then they changed the title, I don't know why. I don't mean to be unenthused."

It wasn't until 1990 though that a movie appeared, directed by Romero collaborator John Harrison, who had recorded the music for both Creepshow and Day of the Dead. Of course, Harrison first came to be known by Romero buffs as the screwdriver zombie in Dawn of the Dead, but went on to work as his assistant director and music provider. By the time of Tales from the Darkside, Harrison was a very experienced major horror player and his direction throughout the three tales, and the linking segments, is superb, providing the thrills, humour and excitement from the word go.

The film starts with housewife/witch Betty (Deborah Harry on great form), about to roast a young boy in her oven. While in the cage however, the boy (played by Matthew Lawrence) cunningly stalls proceedings by telling her three chilling horror stories. The first one, written by Michael McDowell, is based on a story by Arthur Conan Doyle. Lot 249 tells the tale of a graduate (Steve Buscemi, the one and only), who get revenge on those who have wronged him by reanimating an ancient mummy to act out his grizzly vengeance. The second, and arguably best tale, is Cat From Hell. With a screenplay by George (from a story by old pal Stephen King), it tells the story of an ageing pharmaceutical tycoon who hires an assassin (played by David Johansen of the New York Dolls) to whack a menacing cat that stalks his home, and has already killed various friends and family members. The cat is getting his own back on behalf of his species, so says the old man, as his company were responsible for the deaths of thousands of cats during their drug experimentations. The hit man thinks the old timer has lost his mind, until he finds himself face to face with the black cat that is. The tale ends in a devastatingly brutal fashion, a classic special effect you have to see to believe.

However, it's the third tale which creeps you out the most and leaves the most lasting impression. It's about a struggling artist who witnesses a murder by the hands of what appears to be a demonic creature. Threatened by the grotesque devil, he swears to never tell anyone about the incident or he will be killed. Soon after he finds his art career taking off. Inspired by the beast he saw that night, his dark work takes the art world by storm. He has, in effect, sold his soul to the devil in exchange for success. The same night he saw the beast, he met a woman and slept with her. As his career ascends, they end up marrying and having children. Years later he tells her what he saw, breaking the promise he made to the creature, only to see her and his children transform into monsters before his eyes. It turns on him, kills him brutally and flies away with the children, where they turn to stone and become gargoyles on the ledge of a high rise building. Written by McDowell, it's probably the best executed of the three tales, although they all have their own merits.

Tales from the Darkside was a success, raking its budget back a few times at the box office. It remains popular to this day and is possibly more remembered than the series that spawned it. Critically it was also very popular, at the time gaining very positive notices. Writing of Romero's segment in the film, New York Times said "Cat From Hell, which has a screenplay by George A. Romero and carries on Stephen King's special love-hate relationship with the animal kingdom. The particulars of the cat's triumph are rendered in new, different and imaginatively disgusting ways. Dick Smith, the reigning king of horrific transformations, was the film's makeup effects consultant."

The secret to the success of Tales from the Darkside: The Movie is in the way it approaches the old subjects but does so in a new, clever and original fashion. The mummy is a creature we've seen since the start of moving pictures themselves, but here it's given an all new sense of spooky charm, especially when it's getting the better of a future Oscar winner of Julianne Moore's calibre. It's the performances also which elevate Romero's section, with Johansen excellent as the hit man and William Hickey delightfully crusty and eccentric as the old man.

OK, so neither the series nor the film are strictly full on Romero projects, but he does have some involvement, which makes it worthwhile for anyone interested in his work.

AN INTERVIEW WITH JOHN HARRISON
(CREEPSHOW, DAY OF THE DEAD,
TALES FROM THE DARKSIDE)

John Harrison did the music for Creepshow and Day of the Dead, then went on to direct the Tales from the Darkside movie. Here he recalls his various adventures with George A. Romero

Do you remember the first time you met Romero?

I grew up in Pittsburgh and was aware of George from the time he made Night Of The Living Dead. I was in school in Boston when that film came out, and I remember seeing it at the Orson Welles Theater in Cambridge. A midnight screening, and the audience was packed. I decided then and there that I wanted to meet this guy from the 'Burgh who had made such a creepy film. When I went back to Pittsburgh, two of my friends and I put together our own film production company to do commercials and industrials and, hopefully, move into dramatic films. We read that George and his then-partner, Richard Rubinstein, were producing a series of sports documentaries for their company, Laurel Films. We cold-called their office to offer our services, and lo and behold, George answered the phone himself. After a brief introduction, he asked where we were. Since we had our offices just up the street, he said he'd be right over. He came into our editing room and looked at a couple of short films we'd made, and before they were finished, he said, "OK, let's work together." That was the start of a great friendship that continues to this day.

How did you end up working on Creepshow?

George's partner then, Richard Rubinstein, called me one morning and said that George was not happy with the Assistant Directors they'd hired initially. Both were very bright and competent professionals, but they came from a more traditional movie-making background. Back then, those of us making films in Pittsburgh were anything but traditional. Richard asked me if I'd come on board as George's Assistant Director. I had no experience doing that and was pretty nervous about the prospect, but Richard assured me that what was most important was to be by George's side and help him communicate to the cast and crew what we were trying to accomplish on any given day. I wasn't expected to know the DGA handbook.

113

Because we were friends, George and I had a great rapport. And it was the best film school I ever could have attended.

What was it like getting the right music, in that comic book style for such a one off film? Was it difficult?

Being George's Ass't Director allowed me to be at his side during the entire shoot, which further allowed me to get into his thoughts about what he wanted to do with the sound of the film. Most people don't know that, although he's not a musician himself, George has an uncanny and sophisticated musical intuitiveness. Back in the day, he used to make up his own scores by editing pieces of 'library cues' himself. That was our original intention with Creepshow. But some of the tracks we acquired were of poor quality, or they didn't really match the film well. Since I was a musician and had some gear, I offered to enhance some of the cues. That led to my writing some cues where needed, and then the theme music etc etc. In the end, I scored most of the film.

We had always intended a tongue-in-cheek style for the score to match the wit of the film itself. Since I grew up with horror films and loved the genre, it wasn't too difficult to mimic some of the sounds and motifs I had heard and loved. And since Creepshow was an anthology film, I had the opportunity to create different styles of music for each 'episode'. (The same approach I took later with my own film, Tales From The Darkside, The Movie.) Furthermore, since I was with George throughout post, I could constantly tweak and revise the cues as the edit progressed.

This must have been an exciting film to be involve d with. What are some stand out memories from the making of the film?

It was a special experience. It was our first time working with Hollywood 'stars', our first time working within the 'studio system' (in post and distribution), it was our first time on a legendary mix stage (Todd A-O in LA) working with people from other classic movies we'd loved. It was amazing to have our work admired and respected by people we'd admired and respected from afar. Even the hours and hours cooped up on a set with a hundred thousand cockroaches were worth it!

How did you end up working on Day of the Dead?

After Creepshow, I moved to LA. George and Richard had, by then, created a TV show called Tales from the Darkside. The had production teams in LA and New York. They hired me to write and direct episodes. Then in 1985, they finally got the financing for Day together, and they asked me to come back to the 'Burgh and repeat the experience of Creepshow. I became George's Assistant Director and then the film's composer.

Did you have guide lines for the music from Romero, or were you free to do what you liked?

Originally, George had a much more elaborate production scheme for Day. So while those plans were progressing, I started noodling some themes and ideas which I would send to him. When the scaled-back version became a reality, I continued to work with that material because George had liked it originally. Like Creepshow, I stayed for post-production, and moved all my gear into a tiny little office below the editing rooms in downtown Pittsburgh where I would 'temp' the score to match the cut going on upstairs. It was a great process. I could write what I wanted, bring it up for George and Pat Buba, the editor, to review, then go back and revise as needed. Basically, George let me write what I thought would work. I don't think he had any pre-conceived notions, although one afternoon we were watching some scenes and new cues I wrote, and he started laughing and said, "John, you're turning this film into a rock opera."

What was the recording process like and getting the right music for the film?

I had all rights to my own music, of course, and published it through my own company, Harbro Music, which then licensed it to the producers. Any library music in Creepshow (there was none in Day), was purchased through the Capitol Records library. The fees and license term were part of any purchase.

As to the recording, I took the temp tracks I'd created myself with my own recording gear in Pittsburgh, back out to LA. My producer,

John Sutton, arranged time at a terrific studio there, Studio Sound Recorders in Burbank, and we moved in for a couple of weeks to record the score with a great engineer named Bill Smith. I performed all the material on various instruments, with the exception of some percussion and some guitar work which was handled by the great Grant Geissman. John and I then mixed all the tracks and took them over to Todd A-O to be transferred and mixed into the soundtrack. I was there for all the lay-ups and the mix, thanks to George. So I was involved from beginning to end. Later, after we'd made the record deal with Saturn records, Sutton and I went back to Studio Sound and re-edited the cues into Suites for the first album release of the score.

What did you think of the finished movie? I think the music adds a lot to the atmosphere. (I also like the homage to Dawn of the Dead's mall music too.)

Well, the reaction to the score has been quite interesting to me. George and I wanted a counterintuitive sound from what might normally accompany such a graphic horror film. My Day score is often lyrical and sentimental. It is not a traditional horror score, and for that reason it was pretty controversial at first. Many fans apparently did not like it. They wanted to hear the usual shocks and stings and creepy undertones, which my score rarely offered. However, over the years, the score has gained popularity. It's been reissued several times, including recently on vinyl. And we've had several sold out shows to promote the film and its score with audiences made up primarily of fans who weren't even born when we made the film. So I guess ultimately the music has some staying power.

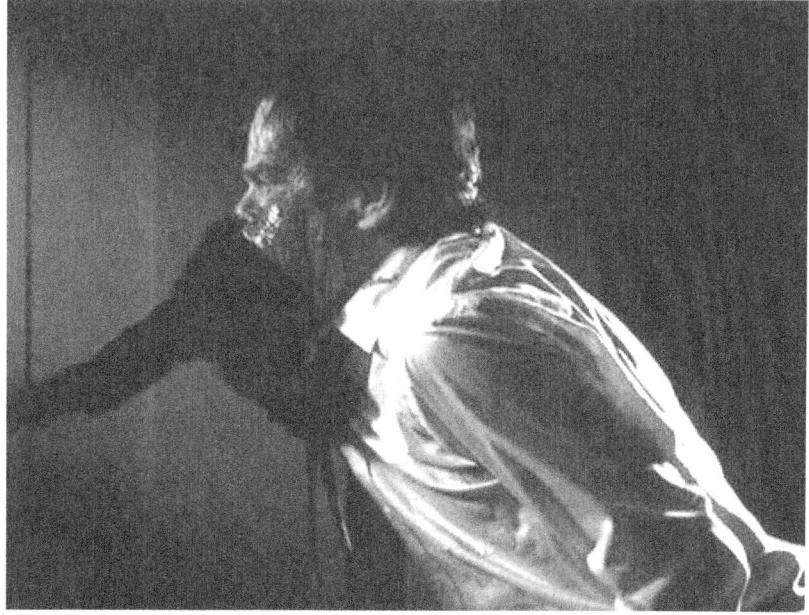

Tales from the Darkside is a real under rated gem I think and your direction is superb. How did this come about for you and was this a good project to be involved in?

Because of my experience with the TV show, producer Richard Rubinstein had thought of me for the feature once he could secure the financing. I was a bit sceptical at first because I was worried it might turn out to be just a slightly enlarged version of the television episodes. But when I read the script and talked to Richard and co-producer Mitch Galin about what they expected, I realized we had an opportunity to elevate the material. And they gave me the resources to put together a fantastic crew of artists to do just that. I loved the experience, and it won me some big international awards.

Did you learn anything from working with Romero for your own directing and writing?

Well, I can't say enough about this. Suffice to say working side-by-side with someone like George was the best school I could have ever attended. The intimacy of day-to-day working through struggles and difficulties that accompany any filmmaking allowed me to learn first-hand how movies really come together. All aspects of them: from the moment of conception, to the scripting, shooting, posting, and exhibition. It was learning by doing, and watching someone as creative as George left indelible impressions on me that helped with my own work.

TWO EVIL EYES (1990)

Outside of his straight forward zombie movies, Romero's career has been very interesting and varied. Addiction and alienation were undertaken in Martin, acting troupes fought for ruler ship in Knightriders and a host of themes and ideas were thrown around in the wonderful freedom of Creepshow. A hidden dark entry in his canon is the 1990 film Two Evil Eyes, a collaboration with horror icon Dario Argento, the very man who had put faith in Romero back in the 1970s and helped him bring Dawn of the Dead to life.

The film received no attention at the time of release and crept out on to video in 1991 in the US. Romero fans were somewhat disappointed by his entry in the movie, The Facts in the Case of M. Valdemar, while some saw it as rather soulless and by the numbers, much preferring Argento's Black Cat tale starring Harvey Keitel.

However, though a minor entry in his filmography, it's still a worthy stop on the Romero train.

Romero had originally wanted two more directors to get involved, to make it a quartet horror anthology tribute to the great American writer Edgar Allen Poe. Apparently these two other film makers were none other than John Carpenter and Wes Craven, and one can only imagine hat a fantastic film that might have been. As it is, Two Evil Eyes remains slightly underwhelming. Had Romero directed his original choice, The Masque of the Red Death - which he saw as a parable for AIDS - the results might have been more interesting. However, the story he did take is rather uninvolving. Romero is a horror master for sure, but horror is not his main focus. He uses horror as a springboard for more important issues and is at his best when providing the scares and the thought provoking themes together in a double whammy. Here, he is lost in a dull horror tunnel with no way out. He is not a student of the genre, as he says himself, so a straight forward horror tale as this is undoubtedly slightly uncomfortable territory for him. There is no passion and it shows.

Roger Corman had deeply immersed himself in the work of Poe in his 1950s and 60s B Movies, and although they were low budget, camp and at times utterly ridiculous, they were also fantastic. You could go as far to say that no one has really filmed a Poe story quite like Corman, despite the creaky production values. All kinds of tributes to Poe have appeared down the years, not just in film, but music too; Lou Reed for instance did a full album on him called The Raven. Two Evil Eyes is respectful to that great story teller, but it's definitely a lesser cinematic adaptation which conjures up little of the mystery and eeriness of the original work.

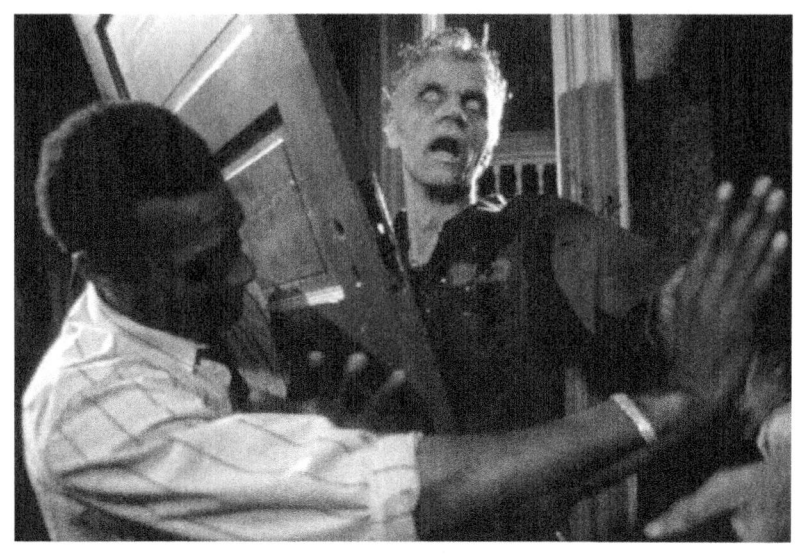

NIGHT OF THE LIVING DEAD:
THE REMAKE (1990)

At least a decade off the great undead revival of the 21st century, zombies films were strictly of the underground in the early 1990s. They had gone through the video nasty era of the late 70s and early 80s, had gone mainstream in Michael Jackson's Thriller and, by 1990, were pretty uncool and admittedly unscary. Vampires were still the in thing, and poor old zombies were left overs, resided to the top shelf of sicko horror and adored by gore nuts the world over. It wasn't the genre for the young, hip and beautiful that's for sure.

Slowly though, the zombie genre started its ascent in the 1990s. Romero's last zombie flick, Day of the Dead, was five years gone and arguably no other undead flick since Dawn of the Dead in 78 had really made a big impact on mainstream culture. Zombies were B movie schlock, daft straight to video trash and grainy European pictures made in the overgrown pubes decade of the 1970s.

One zombie gem which did emerge slightly above soil level was the remake of Romero's 1968 classic Night of the Living Dead, directed by none other than Tom Savini, the man who had made his name doing make up effects for Romero himself. The remake came about when the creators of the original, including Romero and John A Russo had become peeved by the fact they weren't getting the financial reward from Night of the Living Dead, because it had never been copyrighted and anyone and their grandma could basically sell, screen and distribute the film with out the maker's consent. And so, the idea of a remake came up.

Obviously Romero was backing the project and he put forward Tom Savini, a man from behind the scenes who had been dying to get behind the camera itself for some time. But Tom was not going to do a straight remake, word for word, shot for shot. There were things he wanted to change. "I had seen Sigourney Weaver as this great woman hero in Alien," Savini told Daily Dead, 'and I wanted Barbara to become a woman action hero, too. So that's when George wrote in the part about her leaving the house, getting dressed in the combat uniform and kicking ass."

For Savini this as something of a dream come true. He had in fact wanted to do the effects for the original, but found himself called to Vietnam before filming commenced. Now, here he was, some 20 odd years later, not only working on the film but directing it too. Not that he had a great experience mind you. He later called it a nightmare, and was upset that a lot of his ideas didn't make it to the final film.

Romero wasn't around to back him, and he clashed with producers. However, the compromises and difficulties are not evident in the final cut. As a remake, Savini's Night is faithful but differs enough to make it a worthwhile update. The gore in the movie is not over the top, and certainly not on the level of the often sickening European zombie flicks of the previous decade or two. Staying true and respectful to the original, the blood doesn't flow too explicitly. Special notice needs to go to the zombies themselves too, which look really good in colour.

Feedback was gruesomely negative. People thought Savini had butchered a classic horror landmark, and saw the whole thing as pointless. Unlike later remakes, such as the ludicrously bad Psycho reimagining in 1998, this one does have its own identity and stands as its own entity. However, this wasn't picked up at the time of release and it was ripped apart (no pun intended) by the critics. Nowadays though, it has its own little cult following and is seen as a valid remake of Romero's classic. Part of me can see why fans of the 68 classic might have a problem with this, as it's nowhere near as chilling or disturbing. For starters, the black and white graininess and its stark soundtrack made the original extra chilling before anything horrific even began. The creatures may have been lacking in rotten flesh make up, popped out eye balls and excessive decoration, but each actor played the part of the zombie so well that you just believed they were dead by body language alone. While the zombies in the remake are rotting before your eyes, they are in colour and clear as day, thus removing a sizeable part of their own mystique and shadowy elusiveness.

That said, the acting is possibly a little better in the remake, on the whole at least. Duane Jones was a tough one to beat, but Candyman star Tony Todd does a fine job of playing the sturdy, reliable hero. And although there is really only one Barbra (Judith O'Dea), Patricia Tallman reinvents the role with style and panache. Her she's not a catatonic victim frozen in fear (after all, Barbra was the proto slasher girl, screaming and helpless throughout the movie), she's a kick ass heroine and just as brave and important as the male lead character. If Romero had Barbra as a useless victim of the zombie attack, he more than made up for it in Dawn and Day, where the females are vital characters. Savini righted that wrong too in his remake, and it's this element which makes it worthwhile and interesting to the modern viewer. These days, people seem more appreciative of the remake (I always liked it anyway to be honest), and finally it's earning its place in the classic zombie movie canon.

THE DARK HALF (1993)

Romero has said that he wanted to make a zombie film in each decade if he could, in a bid to reflect the times and changes in the social landscape. Unconsciously, he first tackled society with Night of the Living Dead, reflecting the anger of the era, the new blood coming in and devouring the old; a time of revolt, rebellion and action. By the 1970s, consumerism had taken over, and Dawn of the Dead rather unsubtly poked fun at this. In the 1980s, the rot had set in and people just couldn't get along anymore. Guys like Romero, who had put so much emotion into the possibilities that the sixties hoped to materialise, were lost in the 1980s. Day of the Dead was released right in the middle of that decadent decade and really summed up the rage and disenchantment of the time.

In the 1990s however, Romero didn't make a single zombie movie, so he didn't get to vent his anger at the way the world was heading. It was in many ways his most obscure decade. He had directed his own segment of Two Evil Eyes, written a story for the Tales from the Darkside movie and made a cameo appearance in Jonathan Demme's classic thriller Silence of the Lambs. But apart from that, not much came to fruition.

"My partner and I had a housekeeping deal at New Line," Romero explained to the BBC, "and we were tied up in development deals at different studios for eight years. We made a bunch of dough but never made any flicks, and when you don't make a movie you drop off the radar."

He did however direct and write a classy adaptation of Stephen King's classic novel, The Dark Half. Released in 1993 by Orion, it was another underperformer at the box office, and came and went with little fan fare. Even today, it's not widely remembered and is never picked out among the great Stephen King movie adaptations. The early King movies like Carrie, The Shining and Salem's Lot are undisputed classics, despite what the author himself may think of them. Since then, many of the adaptations have been a little creaky, at times iffy and often plain bad. TV mini series versions like It and The Stand were great, and perhaps, as King himself has noted, the TV series is the best format for his work. His novels are vast, there's no other way to put it, and often are so compressed in their movie form that they lose a lot of their meat. Misery, released in 1990 and starring Kathy Bates as the super fan from hell, made a fine transition from the page to screen, and to this day seems to get singled out as one of the best movie versions of a Stephen King book.

The Dark Half, despite being directed by one of King's favourite horror film makers and an old cinematic collaborator, is somewhat buried in time.

It isn't a stretch to say that all of Romero's films are worth watching. Even his lesser works contain clever dialogue, decent performances and an intriguing vibe that pulls you in from the word go, yet it seems that really only his zombie films have made it into the wider public consciousness. This is unfair, for George is not just your average horror director. He's a great film maker, makes interesting character studies and always gets you inside the action, whether it's dramatic or gruesome. It's almost as if he's something of a frustrated director, a visionary who is always having to stick to the genre that they will let him do. Unfairly, as the guy that invented the modern zombie flick, he's seen lesser film makers get the big budgets for their zombie rip offs, while he struggles to scrape together a passable amount of money to bring his own small visions to the screen. It's inevitable that he feels irritated that he is, in effect, shackled to a genre he doesn't even consider himself a student of.

"I'd love to be able to go in and pitch another kind of film and be taken seriously," Romero told Horror Movies website, "but I'm generally not taken seriously. If I were to walk in there with a little romantic comedy, they'd say, What? So that's a bit frustrating because you don't grow up wanting to be a horror filmmaker. You grow up wanting to be a filmmaker and I wish I had a wider range. And I tried early on to do several films that were not genre and nine people saw them, so I don't have the credentials in that regard. There's a bit of frustration there but on the other side of that coin, and far outweighing it is the fact that I've been able to use genre fantasy horror and be able to talk a little bit about- – express my opinion, talk a little bit about society, do a little bit of satire and that's been great, man. A lot of people don't have that platform. So I don't know. I joke and say maybe I'm the Michael Moore of horror but it's wonderful to have that ability. It's sort of my niche. I can go in and do what I want to do."

Although still horror, The Dark Half is not a zombie film and in some ways it gives Romero a chance to flex his directorial muscles in a slightly different field. It's about a novelist (Timothy Hutton) who pens thrillers under the name George Stark, but wants to be taken seriously as a high brow writer. When he literally buries his pen name in a strange almost ritualistic experience, it becomes a life form in its own right, terrorising and killing his friends and associates. Despite the fact that the killer is his secret twin, it's quite literally the story of a writer frustrated with his commercial identity and public persona, a persona so strong that when he attempts to lay it to rest, it comes back for bloody revenge. King, who never really labelled himself a horror writer, must surely have seen himself in the role, or an element of himself at least. After all, he had written novels under the name Richard Bachman in the 70s and 80s, and wrote The Dark Half when it became public knowledge that he had been Bachman all along. Was the pen name liberating for a man tied to straight horror?

If we are seeing King as a man tormented, for want of a better word (perhaps niggled is more fitting), by his literary horror reputation, then we can also view Romero as the troubled horror film maker. Here is a man who wanted to get into film because of seeing Tales of Hoffman, and got his chops directing commercials and working on

Mister Roger's Neighbourhood in the 1960s. When the subject of horror comes up in interviews, Romero usually looks disinterested and repeatedly proclaims that he is not a big fan. He detests modern horror and the torture porn craze, thinks running zombies are ludicrous and feels that horror without subtext is kind of pointless. He has a point, but he also knows that he can only really get a project off the ground if it's in the horror field, and more so if it's a zombie flick. Although I am a horror fan myself, I completely agree with him about the sickeningly graphic schlock coming out these days, and can perfectly understand his frustrations as a director.

As a straight forward horror thriller, The Dark Half works very well and it is a faithful adaptation of King's book. Website The Daily Dead certainly saw it as a film deserving of a reappraisal. "Visually, The Dark Half may look like atypical Romero due to its slick studio polish," they wrote, "but it's a Romero film through and through. His work has primarily examined the dark side of human nature, and The Dark Half takes that idea and makes it literal. It's rough in spots—Romero himself has expressed dissatisfaction with the effects added to the climax after an early test screening—but it remains an exceptionally well-crafted film that faithfully brings King's prose to life in a way so many adaptations of his work fail to do. As we get further away from the 1990s—a decade notoriously difficult for horror—there's hope that The Dark Half starts to be recognized as both one of the better Stephen King adaptations and one of George Romero's most overlooked films—maybe even his most."

For George though, an independent soul to the core, it wasn't a very happy experience. As is the case when he rubs shoulders with the mainstream film business, there was tension. "The Dark Half was the biggest overall (budget)," he told the Telegraph. "I had such a bad experience with that. Orion was supposed to be the filmmaker's studio, but I had bigger trouble with them than Universal. I was terrified of Universal! But Orion were really terrible to work for. It was really tough."

If you ignored Romero's past work and put it out of your mind completely, and put aside the fact that he had a bad time making it, The Dark Half is a really good film and is up there with the best of the Stephen King films. Obviously, as a friend and past collaborator, Romero knew exactly what King might have wanted out of a big screen upgrade, and he keeps the tension, fear and helplessness, often so evident in Stephen's work, constantly to the forefront.

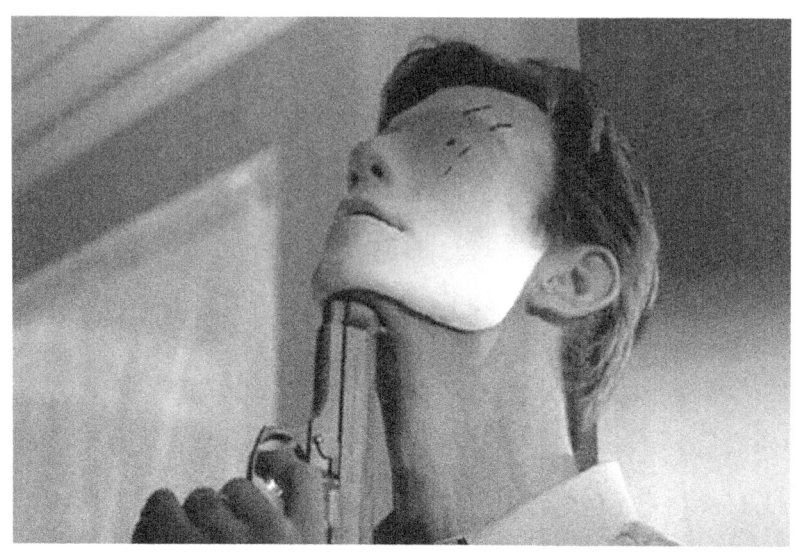

BRUISER (2000)

Sick of the delays and limitations set upon him in the 1990s, Romero was itching to get out there and make a film on his own accord. Having directed a Japanese commercial for the popular Resident Evil computer game, he had also penned a script for a film version, but it was turned down. (The creator of the modern zombie turned down for zombie video game movie adaptation? It figures.) He was also lined up to direct a remake of the classic Mummy tale, but this didn't come to fruition either. Romero was, in two short words, pissed off.

Unusually for the time, Romero chose to shoot his new project in Toronto (where he now live) rather than Pittsburgh. For George, it was a natural move, especially in a financial sense. "What happened in Pittsburgh was, for a while there, it looked like it was going to become a production centre," he told the AV Club. "The city was talking about building stages and stuff, because man, there were a couple of $400 million years. I mean, big movies were coming there to shoot. But all of a sudden it dried up! I was used to working with friends and a sort of family of colleagues, and everybody moved away in order to get work. So that was one of the reasons I left. And then the first film that we shot in Canada, Bruiser, we had a limited budget, but in Canada, we were able to get 20 percent extra on the dollar. So we went to shoot there, and I just fell in love with it. Fell in love with the crews, and just loved working there. Again, sort of having a family of people that you really enjoy working with. I just love working there."

In the film, the great Jason Flemyng stars as Henry, a quiet everyday guy who wakes up to find his face has vanished. Stripped of his identity, Henry plots revenge on all the people who trod on him over the years. After living so long according to the conventions of modern life, he goes ape and throws the rule book out of the window.

Romero had been inspired by Franju's Horror Chamber of Dr Faustus, stirred by the very idea of a blank face, quite literally devoid of any features or characteristics. He saw the plot as a metaphor for alienation, disenchantment with society and the everyman on the street. Again, Romero delivers a thrill packed plot, not free of its own cringe worthy moments of terror, but laces it with themes we can all relate to. Most men at one point in their lives have felt like they are on the outside, maybe briefly lacking their own sense of themselves. Although Romero's message here is as obvious as the consumerism parable of Dawn of the Dead, the blatancy is effective and thought provoking. What is a face? Just a collection of facial features, ticks and movements? Or is it something more? Perhaps it defines who we are, not only to ourselves but to others too. Imagine not having a face, and wonder how different your life would be. It's a fascinating idea, and Romero uses it niftily in this slick, gritty revenge flick.

"I've been working the whole time," George said in one interview upon Bruiser's release. "Just not producing anything. We had a two year deal at New Line. We had a three year development project that went to two different studios. It's just been a nightmare. Hollywood development stuff. Writing draft after draft to the point where you lost interest in it. So I've decided to go back to the roots and do something smaller and more personal."

On the smaller and more personal film in question, Bruiser is actually quite close to Romero's 1977 classic Martin, in that it follows the male outsider through his struggles on the fringes of society. Whereas Martin was a cold hearted blood sucking killer in a run down, back end of nowhere town, Henry is a man who has had enough of going down that narrow goody-goody path and wishes to get his own back on all the bastards who've done him wrong. It's an idea we can all relate to for sure. To Romero, he was a man who winds up "getting shit on so much that he comes to believe he has totally lost his identity. He becomes fearless. I don't think he really is. It's more like Martin, where it's probably in his head."

Romero handles his more psychological material with expertise and never really gives us valid, reasoned explanations for the goings on in the plot or the minds of our antiheroes. We go along with him on his journey of highly unorthodox self discovery, but are never led to either judge or side with him. So is the key to Romero's success on a visual and dramatic level. He never emotionally manipulates or leads the viewer down his own desired paths. We are left in the open to make up our minds. In Bruiser, he hasn't literally lost his face. Henry truly believes he has, so we are invited to go along with him in this deluded assumption. In truth, I see it as a symbolic rebirth, a stripping back, quite literally, and shedding of the skin, to make way for a new man, a new beginning, and a new way of life.

I also feel that Romero is using the opportunity to have a stab at modern society. As he had to comic effect in Dawn of the Dead, Romero again hacks away at our materialistic obsessions and the human being's arrogance and self importance. Corporate bullshit, greed and pressures of middle class life are jabbed and Henry exorcises our collective disdain in the most brutal of fashions. We wouldn't do it ourselves of course, but Henry is cleansing himself, and for some reasons we don't really mind. Such is Romero's genius at making us care for his characters. They are real, not cardboard horror film clichés. Bruiser's Henry, considering Flemyng's portrayal and Romero's detailed writing, is one of his great lost characters.

Like a lot of Romero's non zombie work, Bruiser was overlooked at the time and went straight to video with little fuss, which is a shame, as this is an intelligent and well thought our story. Some sixteen years after its muted release, few pick Bruiser as a Romero stand out, although it does have its admirers. Dread Central for one champion the film on their website, writing "Bruiser never really found its audience and, ten years later, seems to have been entirely forgotten. And while I realize that I'm in the minority here, I've always considered this one to be a bit of an overlooked little gem. It's a showcase for Romero's surviving abilities: razor sharp wit, pitch-black humour and his knack for societal scrutiny. In short: all the things he does best."

LAND OF THE DEAD (2005)

OK, we're well into the new millennium, it's a post 9/11 hell of a world and George W Bush is still in power. Surely, what we all need is a good slice of George A. Romero zombie satire to ease the pain of these modern times. In 2005, that is precisely what we got, and it was definitely worth the twenty year wait since Day of the Dead in 1985.

With a budget in the double figure millions, this was by far the most expensive of Romero's zombie films, although calling them zombie films at all seems to limit their scope and ambition. "The thing is," Romero told Film Four, "I never thought of them as zombies at first. Back in the 1960s, if you said 'zombie', you thought of the guys connected with voodoo. So when we were making Night, I always thought of the monsters as ghouls more than anything else. Then, after Night became a success, critics were writing about how I'd 'redefined the zombie' and I thought 'Did I do that?' I certainly didn't set out to do it, but I just went with it in the end."

Zombies or not, these undead creatures were back again and this time they were not so much stumbling, but marching through the arena of the mainstream. The sets were bigger, there was more a lot more money and it seemed like a better time than any to be angry about the state of America. Land of the Dead continues the tale of the first three flicks, in that the Earth has become infested with the living dead, and the humans that are still around are struggling to get by and most importantly, to get along. Here, the rich are cosy and safe in their lavish living quarters, Fiddler's Green, but down in the streets the working classes are either homeless or running around doing lackey work for the powerful ones at the top. If all this sounds close to reality, then Romero made his message clearer than ever.

Dennis Hopper plays Paul Kaufman, the ruler of the city who has put up the cash for a super tank vehicle called Dead Reckoning, designed by Riley (Simon Baker), which is sent out on missions into the danger zones for supplies and essentials. After becoming disenchanted with the snobbery and class rulings at Fiddler's Green, Cholo (John Leguizamo) hijacks Dead Reckoning and swears to destroy the high rise haven unless Kaufman hands over the cash. In a great side plot, super intelligent zombie Big Daddy (Eugene Clark) is leading a group of the undead straight to Fiddler's Green, gaining more knowledge and human capabilities as they progress.

Once again, Romero delivers his message with anger and precision, and although it might be dimmed a little by the big budget action scenes, gore and showy performances from his famous cast, it's a point the viewer needs to acknowledge in order to feel the film's full impact. This is a class war no doubt, and rather chillingly it mirrors true to our real life society structure. The super rich and powerful are always OK, regardless of inflation and the changes of the times. Ever smug in both the real and Romero's world, they quaff their champagne and use the "lesser" mortals as glorified slaves to act out their schemes in return for spare change. The workers are out there risking their arses, and getting very little in return. Land of the Dead makes this clear time and time again, with Hopper brilliantly slimy as the heartless, greedy leader, out for himself and his rich cohorts. Romero had poked fun at our obsession with materialism in other films, and he had seen a new world order devouring the old guard back in the late sixties. But here, he was taking on modern America with a vengeance. More than ever, his work was relevant and meaningful. It may all have been disguised as a glossy Hollywood production, but beneath the effects galore is a savage attack on the powers that be.

"Originally, I wanted to follow on from the first three films, which had covered the 1960s, 1970s and 1980s," Romero said in one interview. "It was going to look at the problems that were affecting America in the 1990s - the way we were ignoring problems like homelessness, AIDS, and the vanishing middle class. Trouble was, I got caught up in lots of development deals that went nowhere, so I missed the 1990s. I didn't finally finish the script until just after 9/11 and, as you can imagine, nobody wanted to touch it then. I left it on the shelf for a while, and then added a lot of other aspects, making it a little more reflective of what was happening right now in the world. The strange thing is, some parts of the script ended up more relevant than I thought they'd be. The idea of an armoured vehicle going into a little town, mowing everybody down, and the people inside wondering why the town's inhabitants might be pissed off at them - that scene was in the original script, it just means a lot more now. "

After scraping around for meagre budgets for past projects, a part of George must have been relieved and over the moon at the chance to let loose with 15 million dollars. After all, this was the man who first put 600 bucks into Night of the Living Dead, made a string of low budget flicks all coming in at under a million and considered 3 million for Day of the Dead a half decent amount. Following the smash success of the 2004 Dawn of the Dead remake and Simon Pegg's Shaun of the Dead, zombies were cooler than ever. They were immediately thrust into the mainstream, thanks in part to the video game revolution led by the Resident Evil computer franchise, and to a lesser extent the films. Though he invented the whole genre, Romero was still the underground genius reluctant to work with the big studios, due mostly to past disappointments and the rational fear of them interfering with his vision. But here he was, well into his sixties in 2005, at the head of a major Hollywood production. The King of the Zombies was finally getting some credit.

"I'm cynical enough that I don't think there's any particular reason or social zeitgeist that brings people to this material," George said in 2005. "One movie becomes a hit and everyone says let's go make a zombie film. I do think the Resident Evil video games woke everyone up to the undead idea that had been lying dormant for a while. Then 28 Days Later and Shaun of the Dead added fuel to the flames. Those plus the Dawn of the Dead remake certainly helped the Land of the Dead deal. We were in negotiations with Fox Searchlight over the original script idea for   Land of the Dead, entitled   Dead

Reckoning, even before they released 28 Days Later, so creatively we weren't influenced by the zombie regeneration. But it was definitely the success of the Dawn of the Dead remake that got producer Mark Canton and his Atmosphere production company interested. They were able to put a deal together with Universal Pictures very quickly as a result."

However, it wasn't to be a totally happy experience for him, and he certainly felt the pressures of the majors breathing down his neck. "Oh it was too much," he told the Telegraph. "I didn't think it was necessary. I didn't think we needed the stars. But I would rather have had five more days of shooting than an extra box of cigars for Dennis Hopper. Poor Dennis – I mean, I love Dennis. But his cigars were a substantial line item on the budget!"

Although still very much a Romero film, Land of the Dead doesn't have the same intense claustrophobia as the older Dead films. Think of the grainy black and white grittiness of Night of the Living Dead and that creepy old farmhouse. Think of the shopping mall, glorious on the surface, but little more than a nicely painted doomed prison. The most claustrophobic setting of all was the underground military bunker in Day of the Dead, with its endless dark caves and clinical white walls, off of which the endless shouting bounces. Here, amidst the huge set pieces, snappy dialogue, familiar faces and CGI splendour, a little of that doomy hopelessness is gone. As far as Romero's nightmarish visions of a crumbled, chaotic society over run by zombies is concerned, Land of the Dead is the most positive and optimistic of all six of the Dead movies. Though Dawn and Day end with the survivors setting off for a new adventure far away (in Day's case, a remote island away from all the trouble), there was no real conclusion, as is Romero's wish. He doesn't like a happy ending on a wide scale, where everything is OK and order is restored. He often compromises by giving a sort of happy ending for a few characters, tidying things up for the viewer who has invested so much time in their plight. In Land, there are people who are still good in the truest sense, folk with morals and decency, and in a way they succeed against the ruthless money machine. Ruining the ending here, they escape the doomed city while the selfish, mean spirited rich get devoured by the zombies in their supposed safe haven. The film also suggests that the zombies are learning to be more human again, which gives the film true optimism. (It reminds one of Stanley Kubrick's declaration that The Shining was an optimistic picture because it suggested life after death.) Big Daddy and his honourable crusade for his sub-breed's justice is a long way from Bub reading Salem's Lot in Day of the Dead, that's for sure.

There is also a final and rather moving moment, a consolation of sorts - or perhaps an understanding - between the living and the dead. Near the end of the film, after the blood bath at Fiddler's Green, the survivors look back and consider blowing Big Daddy and his followers away into oblivion. After a moment, they decide to leave them be, for as explained by Simon Baker's character, they're just like them - looking for some place to go. This scene is key in understanding Romero's somewhat sympathetic view of his zombies. They are not grizzly, villainous monsters anymore. They are victims too, the biggest victims in fact, of this unexplained, apocalyptic outbreak. There's a mutual respect here that is actually very touching. The film concludes with the consideration that we are all in this great struggle together; black or white, living or undead.

Land of the Dead is immensely enjoyable and stands as its own beast in the Dead movies. It is in many ways the hedonistic entry in the series, the commercial, expensive, lavish extravaganza in a line of low budget, underground grot fests. It's not short of its own amount of gory deaths and zombie munch-a-thons, but it's definitely more toned down than the others, despite some very imaginative demises. (The zombies pulling out a woman's belly button ring is quite vile.) Comparing it to the vile, foul mouthed, gruesome delights of Day of the Dead and it couldn't be more different. Alas, it exists in its own little world.

Seeing Dennis Hopper in a Romero film is a genuine thrill too, not least because Hopper happens to be one of my personal favourite actors. Sure, Romero had had famous names in his films before (Leslie Nielsen and Ted Danson in Creepshow for instance), but it was often before they had found fame (Ed Harris in Knightriders). Seeing a legend of Hopper's stature in the film though lends it a certain amount of class and, dare I say it, dignity.

"Well, Easy Rider came out the same time as his first film," Hopper said in one interview. "They both came out in '69. We both made them in '68 and we both wrote them in '67. They're the same sort of pattern. George is a historic figure in film in my mind, the whole genre of zombie movies. Also the political references that are always inherent in his work. This is really something special. It's really special."

Although primarily seen as a zombie spectacular, and perhaps closer to his earlier vision for a Zombie Gone with the Wind, Land of the Dead is not really that concerned with zombies at all. Again, they are an aspect of the plot, one of the dangers of this drastically altered world, but they are not the primary focus. As they make their way for Fiddler's Green, the intelligent army of undead are becoming more and more human, suggesting the scientific experiments which Logan was exploring in Day of the Dead were not entirely misguided.

As we know, over the years society develops, evolves and moves on. I feel Romero is pointing this out again in Land of the Dead. He was adamant that the new generation was eating up the old in Night of the Living Dead, so who is to say that the zombies of Land of the Dead are not doing the same? The vile financial gluttony of corporate America was at its all time high in 2005, and Romero clearly longed for a big change. Although he never came out and said it was a blatant attack on the republican party (Dennis Hopper, who had once been of the left and had gone over to the right, certainly didn't seem to think it was either), it is a statement about the coldness and smug complacency of the mega rich, a world where the poor and suffering becoming little more than stats and figures.

In Land of the Dead, you could even go as far to say that the zombies are the only real good guys. After all, they are only driven on in their mission by a primal urge, not by greed, arrogance or ego. Big Daddy and his accomplices are not merely scary, threatening devices used to send shivers up our spine in between the plot and dialogue. They are note worthy cast members in their own right, as valuable, if not more so, than the humans who squabble and fight over money, safety and status throughout the picture. There is a revolution happening and the undead want their share of the pie. In many ways, Land of the Dead possibly has more subtext and hidden meanings than any of the Dead films. It can be taken and enjoyed as straight forward horror entertainment, but you'd be wasting a good opportunity if you ignored the messages being sent to us by Romero.

Box office was very healthy for Land of the Dead, and reviews were mostly positive. "Clearly it is high time for these newcomers to stand respectfully aside and allow another appearance from that maestro of the undead, George A Romero," the Guardian wrote respectfully, "whose trilogy Night of the Living Dead (1968), Dawn of the Dead (1978) and the less admired Day of the Dead (1985) has made him a big enough brand to have his name above the title. It is tempting, and enjoyable, to read this movie as a comment on race and class in America: the zombies are leading a kind of unending, futile spartacist uprising against the Wasp rulers in their shopping malls and thousand-dollar suits. On the other hand, the zombies could be a comment on undead America - the cultureless, valueless service-economy drones in their trailer parks and project housing."

Long time Romero supporter Roger Ebert was perhaps a little disinterested in the zombies themselves and saw much more appeal in the cut off, over privileged world of Fiddler's Green. "It's good to see him (Romero) back in the genre he invented with Night of the Living Dead," Ebert wrote, "and still using zombies not simply for target practice but as a device for social satire. It's probably not practical from a box office point of view, but I would love to see a movie set entirely inside a thriving Fiddler's Green. There would be zombies outside but we'd never see them or deal with them. We would simply regard the Good Life as it is lived by those who have walled the zombies out. Do they relax? Have they peace of mind? Do the miseries of others weigh upon them? The parallels with the real world are tantalizing."

144

While Land of the Dead is seen as something of a disappointment to many of the hardcore original trilogy buffs, it's by far the best zombie film made in the 21st century. Intelligent, creepy, funny, action packed, creative, well acted, well directed and wonderfully shot, it's far superior to the vast catalogue of Romero zombie rip offs that have come in the past couple of decades. So if you are going to watch a modern zombie movie, make it one from the old master's lens.

DIARY OF THE DEAD (2007)

Romero sure didn't wait another two decades to execute his next instalment in his Dead franchise, and within two years Diary of the Dead was released. Just before "found footage" movies began getting weekly releases, he opted for a movie shot by its cast, a video diary of sorts. Romero's film is reaction to the web explosion of the new millennium, where everyone is a potential reporter, blogger, newscaster, voice for the people and internet celebrity. George neither celebrates nor condemns this new age, he just shows it as it is.

After a grizzly scene where zombies kill reporters and ambulance staff during a TV news filming, Diary of the Dead begins with a bunch of students making a horror flick in the woods. There's a hilarious little in joke in this scene, when the guy playing the mummy chasing the girl starts to run for her. No, the director exclaims, a corpse wouldn't be able to run so fast; he's dead and his ankles would snap. It's a knowing wink to the sudden crazy wave of running zombie flicks to be spawned by the Dawn of the Dead remake. Back in the movie, the students hear about the outbreak of corpses getting up, coming back to life and devouring the living. Chaos ensues and the friends get their stuff and pile into their van to get back home. The following film is a shaky, though still well shot, exciting, funny, sharp and thrilling adventure, not short of satirical jibes and in jokes.

The thing with George is he will only ever approach doing a Dead film when he feels fired up by something, or if he has something of relevance to say. George was clearly impassioned by the internet phenomenon that seemed to have sprung up from nowhere. Had the web become the first stop for a mass of bored pawns being suckered into social media and You Tube? Well, it's not quite so black and white. Romero can see the good in a world now connected from every angle, but he sees the dangers too. He points out the voyeuristic, morbid curiosities of the everyday citizen, both as viewer and camera toting capturer. Everything is filmed, documented and potentially put online for the world to see within minutes. Is there now too much information? Too much choice? Too much so called education? An overload of waste text and imagery?

"I made a film just a few years ago called Land of the Dead," George told Cinema Blend. "It was the fourth zombie film that I made. I was pretty satisfied with it. I know that some of my fans were not, but when I looked at it, it seemed so big. It was Thunderdome and I didn't know where to go from there. At the same time, actually before we shot Land of the Dead, I had this idea that I wanted to do something about emerging media. I thought, well that's a way to get back and do something really inexpensive and simple and see if I still have the chops and the stamina to go make and make another little guerrilla movie and relate back to the origins of the thing. I had this idea that I could use film students out shooting a school project and zombies begin to walk and they document it. I wanted to do this subjective camera thing before I knew anybody else was working on it. I didn't know about Cloverfield or anything else. I thought we were going to be the first guys out there with one of these."

The clever thing about Diary of the Dead is how it goes way back to the start of the zombie outbreak and shows us a set of people experiencing the horror at the same time as Barbra and company were in Night of the Living Dead. Inconsistencies in technology, like the fact that in Night they are watching crusty old news casts on an old TV compared to the high tech gadgetry of Diary, can easily be overlooked pretty quickly. Romero called it a "rejigging of the myth," so although we hear snippets of original news pieces from Night, this is like starting all over again, while still staying respectful to the original.

The characters in Diary are fantastic and although all are played by little known actors, George makes you immediately warm to them. In fact, the lack of a familiar face actually makes it more interesting and open for the viewer. The menacing appearance of Dennis Hopper, a man so embedded in our collective as the premier 90s villain in Speed, Waterworld and Super Mario Bros, immediately brought on a sense of distrust from his first scene in Land of the Dead. Simon Baker was immediately likeable and John Leguizamo, you just knew it, would be the rough and ready rogue. Here though, with people you've never seen before, you are free to make up your own mind about the characters. It's a credit to the cast that they never come across as corny or wooden, as actors so often do in horror and especially these type of found footage films. But calling Diary of the Dead a horror film is selling it short. This is a thought provoking statement from a man who's been pointing out society's ills since the late 1960s. His is a consistent voice, and from the word go we know are watching a Romero film. It just feels like one and his intelligence as a writer separates him from all the other hacks who are churning out zombie flicks for a cheap buck.

It's clear from reel one that Romero wanted to strip things down and go back to that gritty way of film making again, after the over blown but admittedly joyous excesses of the last picture. It was shot speedily with hand helds, and to make the shoot even quicker he opted for CGI effects for gun shots and zombie deaths. Though you miss the grizzly effects of Savini and the old masters, not for a moment do you believe you are looking at computer generated blood. The secret to CGI is using it economically and as a tool for the film making process, not as the predominant feature. George nails it here, and each zombie death is creative and fresh.

For George though, this was primarily a great opportunity to point out the over exposure on the net and the unstoppable flood of opinions, information and bile on the net. "Is it information or is it opinion and perspective?" he told Cinema Blend. "What the Internet's value is, is that you have access to information, but you also have access to every lunatic that's out there that wants to throw up a blog. Anybody with a radical idea, if it sounds halfway reasonable, is all of a sudden going to get millions of followers. If Hitler were alive today, he wouldn't have to go into the town square, ever; he'd just throw up a blog. People are so used to trusting what comes over that box. People are so used to listening to that shit. They would rather have someone tell them how to think than do their homework and figure out what they should really think. And that to me is the really scary thing. I guess if I were to indict anyone it'd be us, us out here, for not paying enough attention. It's easier to look up from your beer and say, Hey, what that guy said, I happen to agree with that. But is it information? It's not information; it's an opinion or a certain perspective on it. In the old days there were three networks and all of a sudden Walter Cronkite is the most trusted man in America. Everybody believes what he says, not even thinking. In those days we

149

didn't even know it was being spun. We were very willing to just listen to it and go along with. I think that same thing is happening today. The problem is we're going along with, not with Cronkite, not with these three guys anymore. We're going along with 500, 1000, thousands of people. Arianna Huffington? It's bad enough I have to listen to her instead of Joe Blow from Cincinnati. Listen, Joe Blow may have exactly the right idea but there are undoubtedly a lot of people out there who don't. I don't know about this, but I'd almost rather be unknowingly manipulated, at least if the information is being managed, than just be subject to this absolute confusion that just turns into noise. It bothers me. I wish that it was truthful but it's not because people are not truthful. They weren't truthful when they ran the three networks and not necessarily everybody's being truthful now."

On top of the points Romero is unsubtly but effectively making, is a thrilling horror drama with a wonderful ensemble cast. Again, Romero has ensured that the strongest role is a female one, and Michelle Morgan handles the part of Debra with assurance. Unlike Barbra in Night, Debra is not a hysterical victim; she takes control of the situation and leads the group all the way through the picture. She's definitely more Sarah/Lori Cardille than Barbra. As a side note, there's a sly little reference to girls in horror movies running and screaming from the monster in the woods. Perhaps this is a self criticism from George, who is forever apologising for underwriting the Barbra role in Night.

Diary of the Dead is almost ten years old now, but it hasn't aged like a lot of films from that time have. The good thing about it is how it manages to make you forget you are not watching a conventionally directed film. The hand held vibe is off putting for about ten seconds. As soon as the dread mounts and the characters start to interact, you ease into the film. Too many movies now are done in this found footage or home camera style out of sheer laziness. Anyone can get a camera, have someone hold it and point it at stuff, or plonk it down anywhere in a shoddy manner, but it almost never makes for a decent film. Where masters like Romero (and indeed M. Night Shymalan who made the marvellous The Visit) succeed in this style is by still making the film visually striking, using the shaky qualities to their advantage. To still retain a director's sensibilities in this potentially ramshackle style is what separates a cheapo from a properly made movie. Romero's Diary of the Dead is being filmed by ordinary folk, but they are film students, which perhaps explains why they capture everything that goes on so wonderfully. The framing is still precise and George keeps the method exciting and engaging until the very last second. Points are made throughout where one can't help but nod in agreement, but they are placed so carefully between the action that a straight horror buff could ignore them and simply delight in the zombie deaths - and there are plenty of those.

At a budget of only 2 million, Diary of the Dead easily made its money back, although it wasn't a massive smash like Land of the Dead had been. Romero was out promoting this one everywhere, but it still seemed to get a rather muted reaction. Over time though, its appeal has grown and it continues to gather its own set of fandom. A lot of the reviews were good and people seemed to grasp what Romero was getting at.

Some publications and websites didn't get it at all though. IGN cruelly called it "A mess of bad dialogue, poor characterizations and mangled pseudo-documentary conventions, Diary of the Dead is an unwatchable entry that should have been made by one of his successors, but feels that much worse because it's helmed by the master of horror himself." The Guardian was utterly dismissive too, writing "At 68, George Romero has returned with another of his zombie movies and this one certainly has its bizarre, ingenious moments. It's a very 21st-century mocu-nightmare about a new global upsurge of shuffling corpses, their appearance being recorded of course by a film school student and his buddies. The opening news-report sequence is very strong. But from there on in ... well, what more is there to say about the zombie genre and its metaphors for our undead society?"

A lot of people were positive about it too, and appreciated the fact that Romero could have gone bigger than Land of the Dead, but decided to go back and start all over on a low budget. Premiere raved about it, calling it "giddy kick-out-the-jams entertainment. Diary takes a tack that's not exactly new, but is new to Romero, and as one might expect, the director brings a sharp and uncompromising new perspective to it."

AN INTERVIEW WITH
SCOTT WENTWORTH
(ANDREW IN DIARY OF THE DEAD)

Had you admired Romero's work before? Horror wise he is one of the truly intelligent filmmakers in my view.

I am not a big Horror film fan -- I think I get scared too easily -- so although, of course, I had heard of George and his work, I wasn't really familiar with it.

How did you end up in the film?

I got involved in the film in what I thought was the normal way; my agent called and said the casting people wanted to see me for an audition. I drove into Toronto and George was there -- which is unusual for a director at that early stage. He told me that he had just seen me play King Henry in "Henry IV, Part I" at Stratford (Ontario) and thought I would be a good choice for the role of Prof. Maxwell. He had me read through a couple of scenes -- I can't remember if George had at this point written the character as British, or if I just dragged out my best Peter O'Toole impression -- but it was all great fun and I went home and as is usual with these kinds of things, forgot all about it. The following week I was asked to come in again for what I thought was a call back. But George didn't ask me to read anything and he just kept talking about the character and what he wanted to do with the film until finally I said, "I thought this was a call back - are you offering me the part?" "Oh my God", George said, "They didn't tell you? Yes, I'd love for you to do it". Then he fixed me with a stare through his coke bottle glasses, smiled and said, "You *do* know this is a horror movie, right?"

Do you recall first meeting Romero? What was he like?

George, it should be said, is the least macabre person you can imagine. With his grey pony tail and glasses, his soft spoken thoughtful manner, he appears to be a professor emeritus from some liberal think tank -- or an aging independent film maker from the sixties. The last thing you would associate him with would be the Zombie Apocalypse.

That was a great ensemble cast I feel. What kind of experience was it interacting with those performers every day?

154

It was great fun to work on the film -- the cast of young actors was superb and George is a fantastic director for actors. He demands an almost documentary style of performance, but at the same time he creates a character (like mine) that is excessive and theatrical and places all his characters in such outrageous circumstances, that there is a nice tension between the style of the story-telling and the events

of the story itself, that was very creative to explore. It was not an easy shoot, however. We had no studio, so everything was shot on location, a lot of it outside, and most of it at night. The cameras would start rolling as the sun set and we would shoot until sunrise, then stagger back to our various homes or motel rooms, rather like zombies ourselves.

Can I ask what it was like to be directed by Romero? He really does capture the excitement and helplessness of the situation but seems also to be a great actor's director. Would you agree?

One of the things that struck me the most about George was how continuously creative he was. When he had a rough cut put together -- this was months after principal photography had been wrapped -- he called me and Michelle into an editing suite, stuck mikes on us and encouraged us to comment in character as we watched the footage. This became the basis for Michelle's character's narration in the finished film. Also, two important sequences were shot after that; the Amish deaf mute Samuel scene and the powerful ending with the hunters and the strung-up zombies. Incidentally, the reason Maxwell only appears in the Samuel scene as a pair of legs under the broken RV is because I was playing Gloucester in "King Lear" at Stratford on the day they shot it (the ONE daylight scene!) so I couldn't make it. But this shows the almost guerrilla-like filming style that I think gives the film its edgy quality.

SURVIVAL OF THE DEAD (2009)

Rabid Romero zombie junkies didn't have to wait too long for yet another Dead follow up - only two years in fact. Unfortunately a large number of them would be disappointed with the resulting film, Survival of the Dead. More of a drama than a horror film, zombie lovers were satisfied by the highly creative zombie kills and human deaths (and their grisliness too), but let down by the plot itself, which some saw as rather silly. For George, the zombies were just one of the problems again; or as he might have put it himself, "the disaster" that gets in the way of the humans and their already chaotic lives and inability to see eye to eye.

The film follows National Guard Sergeant Crockett (Alan van Sprang, who appeared in both Land and Diary of the Dead too, albeit briefly in both) who ends up on Plum Island in the middle of a feud between two Irish families; the Muldoons and the O'Flynns. (And you can't get much more Irish than that). They see the zombie apocalypse a little differently on this island. Rather than shoot them in the head and dispose of them as the inlanders do in the States, these guys want to keep their infected relatives alive, helping them still serve a purpose in daily island life. Only Patrick O'Flynn (played by Kenneth Walsh) disagrees with the way things are run and wants to destroy all the undead, no matter who they were when they were alive.

Romero has developed the zombie world to a new level here and rather interestingly makes us care for the zombies like never before. No longer are they mere puss bags driven by the urge to eat the flesh of anyone in their path; they are now a part of the problem as opposed to being it. The tagline for the movie, "Survival isn't just for the living" kind of sums the whole movie up. Though taglines are usually no more than a bit of lazy promotional blurb, this one defines the film's aims. There are basically two sides here, with the zombies wedged between the two warring families. Although it often veers into comedic Father Ted territory from time to time, the cast handle their roles well and there is some superbly acted tension. The script is sharp, moving and funny, while the pace is brisk and involving.

Unfortunately, Survival of the Dead didn't get a positive reaction from the critics or most Romero fans. Massacred in some parts of the media, they saw it as the corniest and least effective of the series. And for me, the word "series" is the key here. Consider for instance the highly popular Walking Dead TV show, which is still going on all these seasons later. There are some episodes where absolutely nothing happens at all, and the movement of a slug might actually be more exciting than the verbal sparring and soap opera stroppiness that fills most of the screen time of the show. I loved the early seasons, but it went off and got lost somewhere, and yet it's among the most popular shows in television history. While Survival may be a little more reserved than its predecessors, at least it stops for a moment and considers a different view of the zombie pandemic, something which The Walking Dead rarely does. if taken as an episode in a series, Survival takes a huge leap in terms of progression. It shows us a dramatic change in the world ruled by the undead. Finally, people are learning to co-exist with them, rather than see them as the deadly nemesis. As Romero often points out, it's your fellow man who is the real enemy, the only true monster.

Survival was another low budget venture for Romero, who actually believes it's among his very best work. "I had this conceit about wouldn't it be nice to do this little collage about what the world is like three months, four months, or five months in," Romero told Screencrave. "And I said well, it's not about the Bush administration, it's not about consumerism, so I just wanted to go with a more generalized theme, which is the enmities that don't die. War, in general, and anger and lack of civility – it seems like all of North America needs to take an anger management course. I wanted this microcosm of what war is, these disagreements that can't be resolved. I mean there's not too much of a zombie story here really, is there? The stories are really people stories. They've all been about the humans and how they respond or fail to respond, or respond stupidly. I don't have a problem with that either; I can sort of leave the zombies in the closet until I'm ready for them, until I have the storyline, then I can say OK boys, let's go. That part's not a problem either."

Going straight to DVD, few people seemed overly impressed and critics were often merciless in their attacks. The New York Post, never one to take horror or Romero seriously, were particularly venomous. "When George A. Romero turned 70 this past winter," they snidely spat, "I hope at least one friend approached to say: Dude, seriously. Enough with the zombies. Yet here comes Survival of the Dead, the sixth in the Dead saga that ran out of life two pictures ago. What Romero still seems really, really interested in is the splattery meeting of bullet and brain, or torsos being feasted upon like pizza at a keg party. We learn that a zombie bursts into flames when you fire a flare into his chest, and that his skull might burst if you spray gallons of fire-extinguishing foam into his mouth. I suppose it's nice that Romero has a hobby, but he couldn't be more of a bore if he were showing off his pine cone collection."

Sites like NPR seemed to think there wasn't enough satire, and that Romero's generalised criticism was aimed at nothing in particular. "Romero busies himself with mild wisecracks," they wrote, "overheated (and terribly acted) family melodramas, and ever more inventive ways to rupture the soft melon of a zombie's skull. In the past, the director has usually had an irreverent response on the issues of the day; Survival of the Dead is the first time in the series where he hasn't seemed to bother looking for one."

Even die hard horror publications, usually respondent to Romero's vision, were less than over impressed. Den of Geek gave it 1 star out of 5, rather unfairly when you consider the film's worth. "It has some fine moments of gore," they rather daftly ended their review, "especially in the fight in the last ten minutes. There's quite nice uses of an axe head, a spike, and various good moments involving bullets and flesh tearing. However, it's all too little too late for a film that falls apart if you look at the plot, the acting, the dialogue or, well, anything else! It lacks the social commentary of the previous entries, suffers from one too many conveniences of storytelling, has a plot that occasionally dips its toe into the depth of interesting and doesn't seem aware that it's teetering on the precipice of comedy. If you liked the previous entries, you'll despise this film with a passion. All in all, an absolute waste."

There then, essentially, lies the problem. If you are the kind of person that gets most of your film enjoyment out of heads bursting, innards being pulled out and extreme gore, maybe Romero's movies aren't for you anyway. Personally, I always find the gory bits in his movies of the least interest to me. Sure, they are often excellently executed (the deaths at the climax of Day of the Dead for instance are some of the best ever put on to the screen), but they are often a dramatic and climatic tool in Romero's grander visions. His films are deep character studies, and the zombie deaths are fun, but only a slice of the whole pie. Romero's scripts are vividly wonderful and his handling of family, trust, communication and tension put him up there with the finest directors of the past fifty years. There's a lot more to it than just smashing zombie skulls.

Survival of the Dead is not strictly a horror film, and even if there hadn't been any zombies in it, it would have still been a good drama. Had the infected not come under the undead spell, maybe some kind of plague or disease instead, the film would have worked as a brutally honest study of division in a community. Perhaps marketing it in the horror genre is what gave the film its kiss of death.

As it is, Romero can only find his relatively small budgets if he's doing a zombie flick, and that is a shame. After all, as a filmmaker he has a gritty and well observed grasp on the human condition, and has repeatedly shown an ability to get to the core of mankind's flaws. I would never call Romero a horror director. Not to put down the genre (I'm a huge fan), but I wouldn't narrow his abilities to one field. Modern horror and Romero are not bedfellows, and perhaps that is why a lot of modern horror buffs have a problem with his movies.

Survival of the Dead may not be his finest film, and is certainly the weakest of the six Dead movies so far, but it still has a lot going for it. So for god's sake, don't write off George A. Romero. Who knows what's next?

GEORGE A ROMERO
FILMOGRAPHY

2009 **Survival of the Dead** (Writer and Director)

2007 **Diary of the Dead** (Writer and Director)

2005 **Land of the Dead** (Writer and Director)

2000 **Bruiser** (Writer and Director)

1993 **The Dark Half** (Writer)

1990 **Night of the Living Dead Remake** (Writer)

1990 **Tales from the Darkside: The Movie**
(Writer of segment Cat From Hell)

1990 **Two Evil Eyes** (Writer)

1988 **Monkey Shines** (Writer)

1987 **Creepshow 2** (Writer)

1983-1986 **Tales from the Darkside** (TV series, Writer and Producer)

1985 **Day of the Dead** (Writer and Director)

1982 **Creepshow** (Director)

1981 **Knightriders** (Writer and Director)

1978 **Dawn of the Dead** (Writer and Director)

1976 **Martin** (Writer and Director)

1974 **O.J. Simpson: Juice on the Loose** (TV, Director)

1974 **The Winners** (TV, Director)

1973 **The Crazies** (Writer and Director)

1972 **Season of the Witch** (Writer and Director)

1972 **Hungry Wives** (Writer and Director)

1971 **There's Always Vanilla** (Director)

1968 **Night of the Living Dead** (Writer and Director)

References and Acknowledgments

I would like to thank Joe Pilato, Lori Cardille, John Harrison, Tom Savini and Judith O'Dea for sharing their thoughts and memories of Romero with me over the past few years.

The following sources were useful for this book and are heartily recommended for any Romero fan:

George A. Romero Interviews, book
The Making of George A Romero's Day of the Dead, book
Speak of the Dead, book
Document of the Dead, documentary
The Many Days of Day of the Dead, documentary
Night of the Living Dead, 40th Anniversary, documentary
The Making of Night of the Living Dead, documentary
The Making of Dawn of the Dead, documentary
The Lost Films of George A. Romero, documentary
American Nightmare, documentary

Interviews with George from such publication as Uncut, Daily Dead and other sources were very useful.

Images used in this book are mostly screenshots used to enhance the overviews of the film in question. Others are presumed to be public domain, as copyright holders could not be found.

ABOUT CHRIS WADE

Chris Wade runs the acclaimed recording project Dodson and Fogg, on which the likes of Scarlet Rivera and Hawkwind's Nik Turner have appeared. He's written books on The Kinks, Madonna, Captain Beefheart, Robert De Niro and many others, and has also released audiobooks of his comedic fiction, narrated by such actors as Rik Mayall. His other work includes Rainsmoke, a recording project with actor Nigel Planer and the ongoing Hound Dawg Magazine,

More info at his website: wisdomtwinsbooks.weebly.com

Email the lad: wisdomtwinsbooks@hotmail.com

Printed in Great Britain
by Amazon

85774788R00098